THE RISE OF BIG GOVERNMENT

Americans tend to believe that their country is very different from Europe. Yet over the past half century they have imported and embraced the most transformative social idea of modern Scandinavia: egalitarianism. Today, the United States is more like Sweden than it is different, dedicated to economic redistribution and to vigorously defending its big government. What price, morally and economically, are today's Americans willing to pay to preserve their egalitarian welfare state? Are they willing to turn life into a fiscal cost item? Will they sacrifice their children's future prosperity to defend their entitlements?

The Rise of Big Government: How Egalitarianism Conquered America pursues the answer to these questions by going back to the ideological origins of the modern, egalitarian welfare state. Specifically, the book asks why this idea has been able to set such deep roots in the United States, a country that is often perceived as fundamentally different when it comes to the role of government in the economy. It is shown that there are more similarities than differences between the welfare state in the United States and its Swedish "template."

This book is essential reading for anyone interested in understanding how the egalitarian ideology conquered the United States, and who seeks to gain a deeper understanding of its strength, its resiliency, and the problems it faces in the future.

Sven R. Larson is an American political economist and policy analyst. His research, which is published in peer-review journals and by free-market think tanks, covers fiscal policy, the welfare state and the application of economic freedom. He is the author of *Industrial Poverty* (Gower, 2014) about the role of the welfare state in the European economic crisis.

Economics in the Real World

For a full list of titles in this series, please visit
www.routledge.com/Economics-in-the-Real-World/book-series/ERW

1 **Education Is Not an App**
The Future of University Teaching in the Internet Age
Jonathan A. Poritz, Jonathan Rees

2 **The Privileges of Wealth**
Rising Inequality and the Growing Racial Divide
Robert B. Williams

3 **Neuroliberalism**
Behavioural Government in the Twenty First Century
Mark Whitehead, Rhys Jones, Rachel Lilley, Jessica Pykett, and Rachel Howell

4 **The Rise of Big Government**
How Egalitarianism Conquered America
Sven R. Larson

THE RISE OF BIG GOVERNMENT

How Egalitarianism Conquered America

Sven R. Larson

Routledge
Taylor & Francis Group
LONDON AND NEW YORK

First published 2018
by Routledge
2 Park Square, Milton Park, Abingdon, Oxon OX14 4RN

and by Routledge
711 Third Avenue, New York, NY 10017

Routledge is an imprint of the Taylor & Francis Group, an informa business

British Library Cataloguing-in-Publication Data
A catalogue record for this book is available from the British Library

Library of Congress Cataloging-in-Publication Data
Names: Larson, Sven R., 1965- author.
Title: The rise of big government : how egalitarianism conquered America / Sven R. Larson.
Description: First Edition. | New York : Routledge, 2018. |
Series: Economics in the real world ; 4 | Includes bibliographical references and index.
Identifiers: LCCN 2017020820 | ISBN 978-1-138-29698-5 (hardback) | ISBN 978-1-138-29699-2 (pbk.) | ISBN 978-1-315-09957-6 (ebook)
Subjects: LCSH: United States–Economic policy. | United States–Social policy. | Equality–United States. | Fiscal policy–United States. | Budget deficits–United States. | United States–Politics and government–21st century.
Classification: LCC HC106.84 .L37 2018 | DDC 330.973–dc23
LC record available at https://lccn.loc.gov/2017020820

ISBN: 978-1-138-29698-5 (hbk)
ISBN: 978-1-138-29699-2 (pbk)
ISBN: 978-1-315-09957-6 (ebk)

Typeset in Bembo
by FiSH Books Ltd, Enfield

To Christina, my dear wife, my best friend, and my one and only love

CONTENTS

Acknowledgments *ix*

1 The problem 1

2 Where it all started 5

3 The Swedish roots of the American welfare state 20

4 Exporting egalitarianism to America 47

5 Problem 1: Fiscal Eugenics 60

6 Problem 2: Slow Growth 79

7 Problem 3: Government Debt 102

8 Conclusion 122

References *126*
Index *129*

Income distribution has the form of a pyramid with a broad basis and a narrowing top. In a democracy with effective universal suffrage, this is one of the explanations why we are steadily proceeding in the direction of government control and direction. Even the conservative and liberal parties will have to become the vehicles for this development, or else disappear from the political scene.

Gunnar Myrdal, 1958

ACKNOWLEDGMENTS

This book would not have been possible were it not for Swedish economist Sven Grassman. As a lowly undergraduate student majoring in economics, I found a true mentor in him and his fearless quest to give economic research a purpose. To him, the dismal science was not just an eclectic exercise in math and correlative statistics. It was a method, a comprehensive toolkit, for making people's lives better.

Sadly, he passed away 25 years ago, long before I had learned to put his teachings to work. He would probably not agree with everything in this book – perhaps he would criticize most of it – but it is thanks to his example as an economist, as a public-policy scholar, and as a man of high moral stature, that I have been able to pursue the research that laid the groundwork for this book.

I am also deeply indebted to James Galbraith, who was kind enough to review an early manuscript of this book. Currently the Lloyd Bentsen Chair in Government and Business Relations at the Lyndon B Johnson School of Government of the University of Texas, Austin, Galbraith is an authority on the subject covered in this book. Anyone interested in economic redistribution, egalitarianism and the welfare state must study Galbraith's decades-long scholarship.

I am sure Galbraith will, as Grassman would, find reasons to criticize my arguments and conclusions. There is nothing wrong with that. A book like this one is not written in pursuit of points of agreement. It is written to add to an ongoing conversation that hopefully, at some point, will influence public policy. Only an informed, civilized and purposeful conversation can do that.

I would also like to thank Michael Tanner, Senior Fellow of the Cato Institute, whose prolific and tireless research continues to inspire me. In the pursuit of the ideas that went into this book, I have also benefited from conversations with Cynthia Lummis, Steve Moore, Dan Mitchell, Ronny Noren, and Eva Schliephake Fidalgo. I also greatly appreciate comments on a paper I presented at the World Interdisciplinary Network for Institutional Research in Boston in September 2016, and comments from an anonymous referee on another paper, published in December 2016 by *the Journal of Governance and Regulation.*

Last but definitely not least, I want to thank my wife Christina, who is blessed with endless patience with my absent-mindedness.

1
THE PROBLEM

In 2014, when I published *Industrial Poverty*, my ambition was to explain that the European economic crisis was more complex, and more systemic in nature, than conventional economic wisdom would suggest. I pointed to several macroeconomic factors that seemed to conspire in bringing the European economy to a halt. My thesis was that this systemic stagnation had systemic causes, and that the welfare state was the main origin of those causes.

In the three years that have passed since then, Europe's macroeconomic ailment has continued, with the perennial Greek crisis as its masthead. My conclusions from then, namely that a large welfare state has negative systemic effects on the economy, have again been verified by a couple more years of suppressed private consumption, anemic GDP growth and the redundancy of up to one fifth of the young workforce.

As much as it is important to understand the economics of the stagnation in the European economy, it cannot explain why politicians would choose to continue policies that, from a dispassionate economic viewpoint, either do not work as intended or have outright destructive consequences. Since it can be demonstrated that the welfare state plays a big role in creating Europe's economic quagmire, the inescapable question is: why would elected officials in so many countries not take the appropriate measures to roll back the welfare state?

This book is an attempt to answer that question, but not as a documentalist endeavor. The purpose is not to present evidence of the actual line of thinking of individual politicians. The scope of this book is instead to show how the ideology behind the welfare state was turned into political practice, how it can conquer an economy – and how its inherent flaws, which brought about Europe's economic stagnation, represent a genuine threat to the future of every nation that chooses to cling to the welfare state.

These problems do not only apply to Europe, but are highly relevant to the

United States as well. In fact, there is a prevailing opinion among Americans in general, and to a large degree among scholars, policy experts and politicians, that Europe's problems are irrelevant to the United States. After all, the argument often goes, we do not have a European welfare state.

Yes, we do. The American welfare state has much more in common with its European peers than what sets them apart. In fact, the welfare state that emerged in the United States as a result of President Johnson's War on Poverty can trace its ideological roots with direct lineage back to the Swedish welfare state, which is often – and rightly so – held up as the most radical of them all. In both ideological architecture, economic execution and macroeconomic effect, the American welfare state has more in common with the Swedish welfare state than it has with, e.g., the British one.

The similarities between the Swedish and American welfare states also mean that the ailments that characterize the former are highly relevant to – and to some degree already present in – the latter. Without a thorough understanding of the common ideological roots between the two, it is extremely difficult to fully grasp the nature, and the consequences of, those similarities.

It is easy to dismiss the shared egalitarian roots of the Swedish and American welfare states as simple rhetoric. After all, in January 2017 President Trump took office and immediately began working on a rollback of many policies from his predecessor. Understandably, a consensus emerged across political dividing lines that America was no longer heading down the welfare state downslope. Quite the contrary: conservatism was now back in charge. In the dust of Hillary Clinton's loss, Democrats were shocked at how voters continued to abandon them, adding a pivotal presidential election loss to the party's decline in the states and Republican majorities in Congress.

On the other side of the aisle, joyous Always-Trumpers overcame their differences with Never-Trumpers and shook hands. They quickly agreed that with Congress behind him, the Donald is going to make America great again – whatever that means – and that the Trump presidency is going to be a conservative victory lap.

Superficially, both sides were right. Secretary Clinton, openly committed to new entitlement programs and higher taxes, was no doubt a representative for a traditional progressive political agenda. From an equally superficial viewpoint, Mr. Trump comes across as a traditional conservative, suggesting that the cheers and jeers from the November election were correct.

However, when Trump is put in his proper context, his victory is no longer the defeat of egalitarianism, and it is certainly not the beginning of the end of the American welfare state. To the chagrin of Trump voters, and to the reassurance of distraught Clinton and Sanders backers, conservatism is not back in charge. Donald Trump will not challenge the political victories that egalitarians have scored since the War on Poverty.

The left, whether they call themselves liberals, progressives or social democrats, can rest assure that their ideological common ground, also known as egalitarianism, will continue to define the American future, just as it has dominated the past several decades.

In short: egalitarianism, the ideology that was imported to America from Sweden to create a platform for the War on Poverty, will not go away any time soon. On the contrary, it will prevail; its political practice, the welfare state, will survive both the Trump presidency and the Republican Congressional majority.

Neither President Trump nor any influential member of the GOP in Congress has the ambition to substantially reform the entitlement programs that consume more than two thirds of the federal budget. Social Security, Medicare, Medicaid, TANF, SNAP, WIC, housing subsidies, and many more programs will continue to exist, dispense benefits and require tax dollars to pay for them.

If anything, Republicans in Congress will work with President Trump to try to make the welfare state more fiscally sustainable.

Simply put: there is no ideological challenge to the welfare state in American politics today, nor is there any challenge in the foreseeable future.

For this reason, it is fundamentally important that Americans of all ideological backgrounds put aside their false notions that this country is too different from Sweden, and Europe in general, to be immunized against the systemic ailments of the welfare state.

Recognition of the cross-Atlantic similarities comes with an assignment: to understand in detail that if the welfare state is going to survive for the foreseeable future, its proponents must address its serious moral and macroeconomic challenges.

The problems of the federal debt and the long-term drift toward macroeconomic stagnation are serious enough to jeopardize the welfare state's future. In addition, it faces a sharp moral challenge from within itself, a challenge that has increasingly put the welfare state at odds with core values of our civilization.

There is limited understanding of these problems among conservatives, primarily the economic problems. So far, though, the left appears unwilling to even recognize the existence of these problems, which begs two questions:

- If left unsolved, will the problems inherent to the welfare state grow serious enough to be the henchman of egalitarianism itself? In other words: will the left pull the carpet out from underneath its own historic political victory by simply looking the other way?
- If America's egalitarians are unwilling to step up to the plate and save the welfare state, is it not logical to bring the entire egalitarian project to an end, roll back entitlements and return responsibilities for welfare, education, health care and income security back to the private sector?

This book will not – and cannot – answer the first question. Only those who belong to the egalitarian camp can do so. What this book can do, though, is provide a detailed analysis of the systemic problems that are built into the welfare state. In response, conservatives and egalitarians can choose to either apply sustainable solutions to these problems, or they can organize a peaceful transition from the welfare state to a genuinely free-market economy with a state strictly limited to its core functions.

Either of these two solutions is better than the alternative: a period of disorderly collapse of the welfare state, hurling us into social and economic turmoil where the future will, at best, be fundamentally uncertain.

2

WHERE IT ALL STARTED

The welfare state was not built overnight. It is the brainchild of a decades-long advance of egalitarian ideas in Europe, from where it was imported to the United States. The welfare state has fundamentally redesigned society and the economy, changed cultural and social values and affected the daily lives of almost every one of us.

Politically, the welfare state is the biggest victory ever for the American left. It redistributes trillions of dollars from the rich to the poor, from the wealthy to the middle class. On a daily basis, it turns the ideology and the values of egalitarianism into economic reality. In the shape of entitlements, taxes and regulations, it has fundamentally redrawn the architecture of America.

Its presence in our society and our economy is so overwhelming, and so entrenched, that no Republican – not even a devout libertarian like Senator Rand Paul – utters a word about doing away with the welfare state. No conservative in Congress has proposed that the United States returns to a pre-egalitarian era.

Part of the reason is, undoubtedly, that up to half of all Americans get some sort of benefit from government. The benefits are often generous: in 35 states, tax-paid programs such as SNAP, WIC, TANF, Medicaid and housing subsidies make life so comfortable that it does not pay to take a minimum-wage job.[1]

Another reason for the lack of challenge to the welfare state is its sheer size. Almost three quarters of federal expenditures are directly or indirectly used for entitlements. In 2015, that meant $2.6 trillion to health care, income security, education, social services, housing and other items for people who, government said, were entitled to a higher standard of living than they could afford on their own. Any reforms to such an enormous amount of government spending would require a very hefty investment by members of Congress and others in crafting legislation and enduring the political battle that could certainly be expected.

There is also a third reason why conservatives plead no contest on the welfare state. The ideological purpose of the welfare state is economic redistribution. Its goal, in turn, is to reduce and eventually eliminate differences in standard of living between Americans. This egalitarian end goal has defined the welfare state since President Lyndon Johnson's State of the Union speech declared the War on Poverty. At the time, conservatives were unprepared for – and under-educated on – the ideological, economic and political force of egalitarianism. Frankly, they never saw what was coming and have never really caught up to a point where they have been able to forcefully, comprehensively and successfully produce a counter-alternative to egalitarianism.

The welfare state's entrenched presence, sheer size and ideological fervor explain why President Johnson became the first truly egalitarian president, but also why others who have followed him in the Oval Office have allowed his egalitarian project to continue. A case in point is conservative icon Ronald Reagan, who as president was a bigger friend of the welfare state than most others: on his watch, spending on economic redistribution increased by 6.7 percent per year.

President Bush Jr. spearheaded the most radical expansion of Medicare in the history of the program. He did so with passionate support from a Republican Congressional majority.

Over the decades, Republicans have successfully competed with Democrats over being the best stewards of the American welfare state. Like Democrats, Republicans defend Social Security and Medicare; if they bring up any criticism, it is concentrated in fiscal sustainability concerns. They take the same attitude to all the programs that were created under President Johnson's War on Poverty; tax cuts, a Republican staple, are never coupled with structural reductions in government spending. The only purpose of those cuts, therefore, is to increase economic growth and thereby expand the tax base for the welfare state. A stronger economy helps perpetuate entitlement funding.

Nothing will change with Donald Trump's presidency. He and Congressional Republicans may twist and tweak programs, but overall they will keep and continue to fund the welfare state just like Congress and the executive branch have done uninterruptedly since Lyndon Johnson's Economic Opportunity Act became law in 1964.

Redefining the purpose of government

That year was a watershed mark in American political history. Up until then, the share of federal spending that was focused on helping the poor had been guided by the economic, social and cultural heritage from the founding of the Republic. Social policies were guided by, for lack of a better term, social conservatism. That all changed with the 1964 Economic Opportunity Act, which marked the beginning of a new era. From that point on, social policies were guided not by principles of limited government, but by egalitarianism. The political spotlight turned from alleviation of poverty to economic redistribution.

The effects of this ideological shift did not materialize abruptly, but became gradually visible as the War on Poverty expanded entitlement programs and reached broader layers of the American people. To the left, it was a victory of political gradualism that slowly but relentlessly gained universal acceptance.

There was opposition to the egalitarian project, but it gradually withered from the political mainstream.[2] Over time, Republicans de facto surrendered – and egalitarians won.

However, their victory is not one of moral, social or economic superiority. Their victory was as much a case of ideological over-reach, a case of not being careful enough about what to wish for, as it was a matter of conservative failure to understand the true nature of the welfare state. When criticizing the welfare state, and the War on Poverty, they explicitly point to the rate of poverty: since a larger share of the American population lives in poverty today than when the War was declared in 1964, critics claim that the welfare state has failed.[3]

This criticism would have been correct if poverty reduction was the right metric for evaluating the egalitarian political project. Yet egalitarianism does not operate by those metrics; the rate of poverty is irrelevant. What matters to the egalitarian is instead the reduction of economic differences between citizens; in its absolute form, egalitarianism is an argument for the complete eradication of any differences between citizens in terms of income, consumption and wealth.

These metrics are to be taken literally. The idea that every man and woman should earn the same amount of money, regardless of profession and performance, is not just a theory, but a guiding principle for egalitarian policy.

As a political practice, egalitarianism is every bit as radical as it may sound. The pursuit of absolute egalitarianism takes revolutionary proportions, eventually altering every aspect of our economic system, from the meaning of property rights to the purpose of the free market.

In order to transform a society and its economy according to their principles, egalitarians build entitlement programs. At first appearance, these programs appear to be innocuous and ideologically harmless. After all, they provide select groups of needy citizens with cash or in-kind benefits. Is it not what social conservatives have always done, too?

The difference between egalitarianism and social conservatism is that the latter used poverty alleviation as a means to preserve and improve a society where individual income was – and should be – the result of individual effort and pursuit of opportunity. Therefore, entitlement programs are constructed to provide a passive safety net, available only as a last resort for those to whom no other means of subsistence is available.

Egalitarianism, on the other hand, replaces the social conservative's absolute poverty concept with a relative one. Poverty is no longer a defined minimum of existence, but a life at a standard that is relative to the economic performance of society as a whole. The immediate, and transformative, consequence of this new poverty definition is that entitlement programs now have a new purpose. Where their job was previously temporary and contingent upon a population living at the subsistence level, they are now a permanent, integral part of government. In fact, under the relative poverty concept they become more relevant as society grows more prosperous: as median income rises, so does the threshold for poverty. With the increase in the poverty threshold, the share of the population defined as poor will also increase – quite the contrary effect from what one would see under the socially conservative absolute-poverty definition.

This effect of the relative poverty concept is no accident. On the contrary, the egalitarian poverty concept deliberately redefines the purpose of government spending: increasingly, fiscal policy drifts away from an economy with limited government. The main purpose is now income redistribution; over time, all other policy goals take the back seat to redistribution.

Taken together, the ideological, institutional and policy elements of the welfare state constitute the egalitarian project. As intended, this project has redefined the social and economic organization of modern industrial societies. Its success lies in its entirety; conservative critics remain fragmented in their criticism of the egalitarian project, focusing on the erroneous metrics of poverty, on the volume of spending, or on the negative effects of high and progressive taxes needed to pay for the redistributive welfare state.

It is almost unheard of that conservatives challenge egalitarianism systemically. Outside of ideological challenges in Robert Nozick's stellar tradition, criticism of the egalitarian project is predominantly concentrated on elements of the government budget.[4]

This does not mean conservatives have been ineffective or without influence in the egalitarian era. They have made a considerable difference, especially in terms of tax policy. Under the banner of supply-side economics, conservatives led the charge against the extreme taxes that President Reagan inherited from President Carter. The tax cuts that Reagan signed into law boosted revenue by means of stronger growth;[5] similar policies had similar effects – though in smaller proportions – under the Bush Jr. administration.

However, the conservative practice of supply-side economics has actually epitomized their surrender before the welfare state. While the success of the tax reforms has been claimed as evidence of the strength of free-market and supply-side economics, at no point did conservatives use that success to challenge the egalitarian project per se. In fact, the success of supply-side economics gave the welfare state new fiscal life; in its absence, the American welfare state would, already in the late 1980s, have fallen into the same economic problems that led several European countries down the road of austerity and stagnation.

The fact that the United States has avoided encounters with European-style austerity does not mean that we won't have such encounters in the future. On the contrary they are increasingly likely, primarily because our welfare state is based on the same egalitarian principles that define Europe's welfare states. The American and European welfare states differ in degree – not in kind – and in terms of the pace of advancement.

The cross-Atlantic similarities also mean that the problems facing the American welfare state are essentially similar to those that Europe's welfare states have been dealing with in increments since the 1980s. These problems …

- A long-term decline in economic growth;
- Structural budget deficits; and
- Policies guided by ethical principles that subordinate the individual to the interests of the collective;

are serious enough that, if left unaddressed, will destroy the very foundation upon which the welfare state is built. In fact, with egalitarianism as the prevailing ideology of our time, there is a formidable weight of responsibility on the shoulders of egalitarians to solve these problems – or else the welfare state's ailments will eventually eradicate prosperity from the Western world for the foreseeable future.

By historic standards, these problems have surfaced relatively recently. The first 30–40 years of the European welfare state's evolution were not characterized by slow growth and chronic deficits. Those problems emerged, on a broad scale, during or after the 1970s, yet it is not difficult to link them back to the welfare state itself.

The same is true for the welfare state's increasingly serious ethical problems.

In fact, the welfare state carries within itself the seeds of its own ailment. To see why, it is necessary to review the historic advancement of egalitarianism and its welfare-state practice.

Egalitarianism arrives in America

The founding of the American welfare state is a matter of dispute in the literature. Some have placed its ideological roots in the late nineteenth century,[6] while others locate it in the Franklin Roosevelt presidency. Falling into the latter category, Walter Trattner, former professor of history at the University of Wisconsin, points to the Social Security Act of 1935 as a milestone in building the American welfare state.[7] His account of the welfare state's history is one of an evolutionary process, from ancient ideas of charity in Jewish and Christian theological practice to government-provided care for the poor in the early twentieth century.

However, Trattner distinguishes between two eras of welfare, separated by the line between the nineteenth and twentieth centuries. He does this while characterizing the Reagan presidency as an era of "war on the welfare state." To President Reagan, the 1800s was the "golden era" of individualism, free enterprise and laissez-faire (Trattner 1999, p. 406):

> This nostalgic view of the past and obsession with self-sufficiency precluded the President from understanding not only the problems faced by the victims of systemic oppression … but the plight of millions of others as well … who were working but who could not support themselves and their families on their meager earnings.

While it may be possible that President Reagan harbored deep animosity toward the welfare state (although Trattner does not provide any evidence) his fiscal policy sends a different message. During his White House tenure, Reagan signed budgets that expanded entitlement spending by, on average, 6.7 percent per year in current prices.

In other words, President Reagan did not reverse America's trend of a growing welfare state. The fact of the matter is that there has never been any such reversal: the only changes that have taken place to the American welfare state is in the pace of its expansion. Overall, it is a continuing project with widespread support in both liberal and conservative circles.

The welfare state's widespread support would be easy to understand if Trattner were correct in his argument that the welfare state is a long continuum of expanding government. His image is one of a centuries-long trend of government increasingly taking on more responsibilities for the poor, the destitute and the downtrodden. Over time, the caretaker role has expanded as the standard of living has increased and more resources have become available for redistribution.

If this continuum were true, it would mean that statism would transcend ideologies, and the welfare state as it were known to Chancellor Bismarck in late nineteenth-century Prussia would differ only in size from the Swedish welfare state as it stood a century later.

The problem is that this statist continuum does not exist. The welfare state that Bismarck pursued was not the same welfare state that Swedish economist Gunnar Myrdal and his sociologist wife Alva envisioned in their 1934 book *The Demographic Crisis*. The welfare state that Lord Beveridge outlined in his report of 1946 to the British Parliament was different in kind from the welfare state that sprung from President Lyndon Johnson's 1964 State of the Union speech.

The fallacy in the centuries-long lineage argument is that it does not distinguish between a welfare state built on conservative principles, and one that rests on an egalitarian foundation. Bismarck, like Lord Beveridge and the authors of the English Elizabethan Poverty Law of 1601, all had the ambition to alleviate suffering among the poor. Similarly, the proliferation of unemployment insurance in the United States during the Great Depression was motivated by compassionate conservatism.

By contrast, Mr. and Mrs. Myrdal, who in their book of 1934 outlined the architecture of the Swedish welfare state, sought not to alleviate poverty but to establish a system of permanent economic redistribution. The goal was not to provide for a person in case he fell into poverty; the goal was to give working people, with steady jobs, steady income and a generally stable life, more money and more resources to spend than they made on working.[8]

President Johnson concurred. He did not wage his War on Poverty to alleviate poverty, not even to eradicate it (even though that was his battle cry), but to sever the ties between a man's earnings and his standard of living. If he earned "less," he would be provided with more by government; if he earned "more," government would take a disproportionate share of his income for the purposes of redistribution.

Behind the ambitions of the Myrdals and of President Johnson lay the ideological principle of egalitarianism, the goal of which is to minimize – and in its absolute form eradicate – economic differences between any two randomly selected citizens. This is an inherent goal, desirable in itself to those who embrace egalitarianism.

It is important not to under-estimate the significance of a shift in welfare-state policy from its socially conservative base to one of egalitarianism. Under social conservatism, welfare programs – and thereby the size of government – are naturally limited: the ambition with government spending is to raise the absolute standard of living of the poor. The object of comparison, in other words the metrics for success of welfare policy, is whether or not the poor have more resources as a result of welfare policy, compared to how they would live otherwise.

At no point does it matter to the social conservative how the rest of the population is doing.

By contrast, under egalitarianism the absolute standard of living of the poor is irrelevant. Here, the metrics of success for welfare policy is to what degree it reduces the difference in standard of living between the poor and the non-poor.

Put simply, yet accurately, the choice is between:

- The poor making $1 per day and the rich making $2 per day; and
- The poor making $10 per day and the rich making $40 per day,

social conservatism endorses the latter while egalitarianism prescribes the former.

By fundamentally rewriting the purpose of government spending, egalitarianism marks a new era for government, and for our Western civilization. Where the socially conservative welfare state was a limited assignment, the modern, egalitarian welfare state is an open-ended commitment to growth in government. For the United States, that open-ended commitment began in 1964 when President Lyndon Johnson explained (emphasis added):[9]

> Unfortunately, many Americans live on the outskirts of hope – some because of their poverty, and some because of their color, and all too many because of both. Our task is to help replace their despair with opportunity. *This administration today, here and now, declares unconditional war on poverty in America.* I urge this Congress and all Americans to join with me in that effort … our joint Federal-local effort must pursue poverty, pursue it wherever it exists – in city slums and small towns, in sharecropper shacks or in migrant worker camps, on Indian Reservations, among whites as well as Negroes, among the young as well as the aged, in the boom towns and in the depressed areas. *Our aim is not only to relieve the symptom of poverty, but to cure it and, above all, to prevent it.*

He also presented his policy arsenal:

- Special help to very under-developed areas such as Appalachia;
- Work programs for the young and "modernized" unemployment benefits for adults;

- Big expansion of the food-stamp program (today known as Supplemental Nutritional Assistance Program);
- A major expansion of the minimum-wage law;
- Federal money for schools in impoverished areas;
- An urban renewal program aiming for "a decent home for every American family";
- More libraries, hospitals and nursing homes; and
- Health insurance for "our older citizens financed by every worker and his employer under Social Security … without cost to the Treasury."

The last point gave us Medicare. President Johnson also signed Medicaid into law, making both programs essential to the War on Poverty.

As these and other entitlement programs went into effect, federal spending began following a new path forward, namely that of economic redistribution. New metrics were applied to the success of entitlement spending, metrics that had nothing to do with the officially stated goal of eliminating poverty.

Many critics of the War on Poverty have yet to understand that criticizing the War based on a trend in the poverty rate is a moot point to egalitarians. Nevertheless, the following data is often used by conservatives and other opponents of egalitarianism:

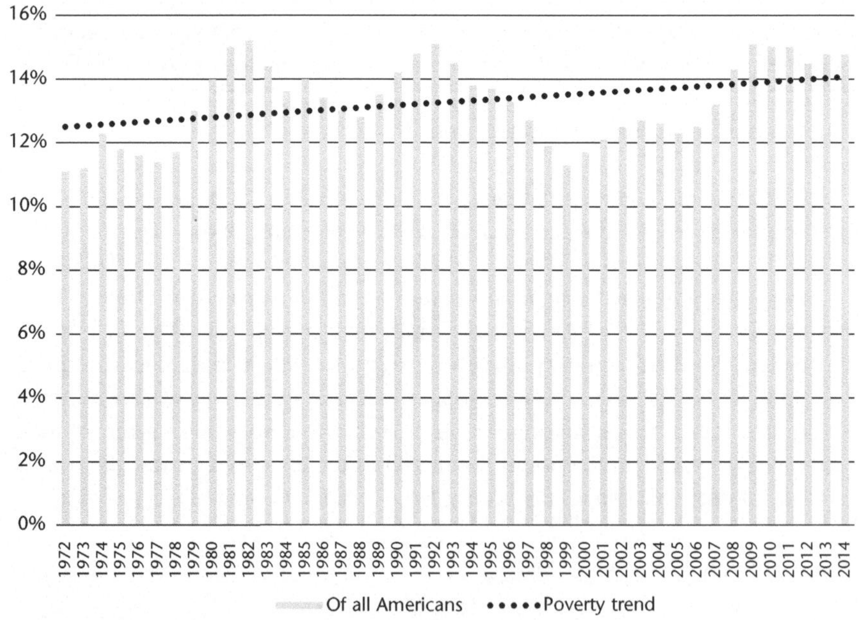

FIGURE 2.1 Percent of population at below 100 percent of FPL

Source: Census Bureau

James Bartholomew, a British writer and fellow of the Institute for Economic Affairs and the Adam Smith Institute, uses this very trend in American poverty to declare the War on Poverty a failure.[10]

Others have concurred:

- Rachel Sheffield, writing for the *Daily Signal* in January 2016, held up built-in mechanisms in welfare programs, such as weak work requirements and strong marriage penalties, as reasons why the War has perpetuated, not ended, poverty.
- In a September 2014 commentary for the Heritage Foundation, Robert Rector pointed out that the sum of all welfare aid in the United States in 2013 was "five times what was needed to eliminate all poverty" in the country.
- In March 2014 Louis Woodhill, contributor to the *Forbes Magazine*, declared the War on Poverty a "catastrophe".
- In April 2012 Michael Tanner estimated that nearly $1 trillion is being spent every year on fighting poverty in the United States, with no success in sight.

In 1998 *The New York Times* sent a reporter to Appalachia, the region specifically mentioned by President Johnson in the Declaration of War. *The Times* described a region that, in terms of socio-economic status, had barely changed at all since 1964.

Not all critics of the War on Poverty are as quick to declare it a failure. A more measured conclusion, reflecting the need for more complex metrics than the poverty rate, is presented in Cato Institute Senior Fellow Michael Tanner's 2014 evaluation of the first 50 years of the War. Tanner and his co-author, Cato Research Associate Charles Hughes, acknowledge that the War on Poverty has indeed alleviated the material deprivations of life in poverty. However, they explain, the benefits from the War on Poverty primarily helped those who were already leading a socio-economically stable life, not those whose lives were burdened by other problems:[11]

> Moreover, other factors like the passage of the Civil Rights Act, the expansion of economic opportunities to African Americans and women, increased private charity, and general economic growth may all have played a role in whatever poverty reduction occurred.

They conclude that "the programs [the War on Poverty] spawned have long since reached a point of diminishing returns."

Understanding the War on Poverty as an open-ended fiscal commitment helps explain the unending expansion of its entitlement programs. The food-stamp program is a good example, with significant increase in enrollment since the program was reformed and placed under the Food and Consumer Service in 1969. The agency is now known as the the Food and Nutrition Service and the food-stamp program has been renamed the Supplemental Nutritional Assistance Program (SNAP). In 2015 it distributed $74 billion worth of benefits to 45 million people.

A comparison of SNAP enrollment and the poverty rate reveals that the goal behind this program is not ending poverty, but economic redistribution:

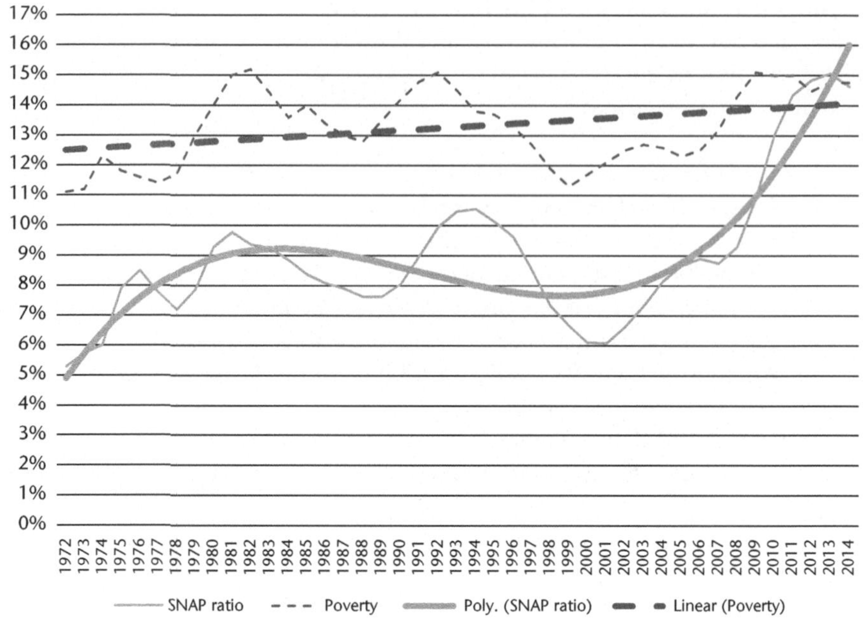

FIGURE 2.2 Poverty rate: SNAP enrollment rate

Source: Census Bureau; Department of Agriculture, Food and Nutrition Service

Today, there are as many Americans on food stamps as there are Americans living in poverty, yet the program is alive and well.

The same thing is true for Medicaid. In the 25 years from 1989 to 2014 the number of poor Americans increased by 15.8 million. During the same time the enrollment in Medicaid increased by a staggering 40.9 million.

Less than half of that increase, 19 million to be exact, was due to President Obama's Affordable Care Act. But what is really interesting here is that every one of the four last presidents has signed budgets increasing Medicaid enrollment more than the increase in poverty (see Figure 2.3).

The key to understanding the egalitarian purpose behind SNAP and Medicaid is in the definition of poverty.

Relative poverty: the key to the egalitarian transformation of America

Historically, the United States relied on an absolute poverty concept, which defines poverty independently of the general standard of living in a society.[12] Prior to the invention of the relative poverty concept, federal welfare programs had been specifically designed to relieve absolute poverty. While those programs expanded

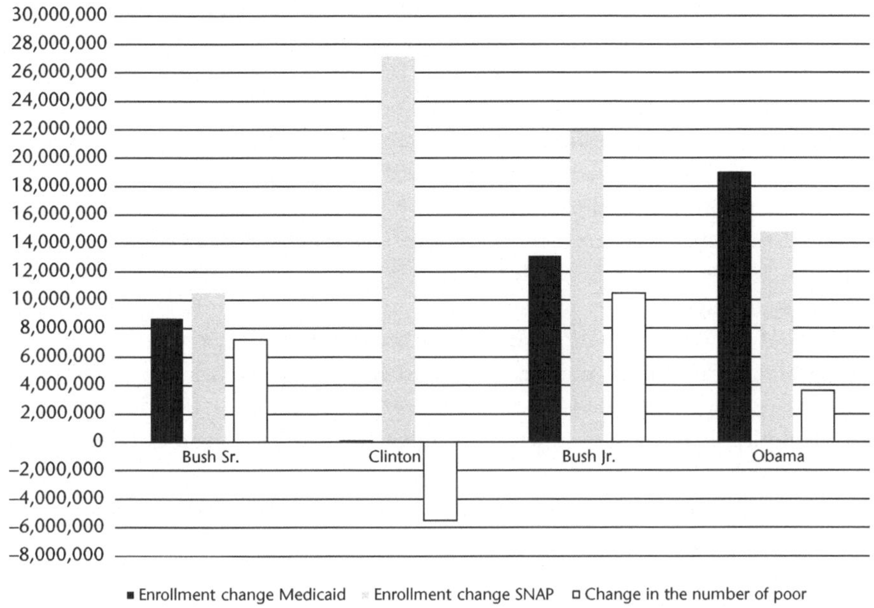

FIGURE 2.3 Change in poverty and in medicaid and SNAP enrollment

Source: Census Bureau; USDA Food and Nutrition Service

radically in the wake of the Great Depression,[13] the purpose, and the definition of entitlements in the programs, were all intended to make an absolute level of poverty as palatable as possible.

So long as government was concerned with providing relief from absolute poverty, its task was limited in terms of spending per poor person. In a manner of speaking, every person who met the absolute-poverty measurement would be handed a basket of food, be granted subsistence shelter and a sparse supply of clothes. He would be granted access to a minimum, life-saving supply of health care and whatever else he needed to survive.

Regardless of one's moral reaction to this concept, it important to understand its practical implications. By putting a limit on the commitment of government resources, the absolute poverty concept necessitates private charities, whether affiliated with churches or entirely secular, and the rest of the volunteer community to provide the bulk of help to those in need.

Because of its natural limitation of government and its encouragement of private charity, the absolute poverty concept is compatible with both traditional, minimal-state libertarianism and socially compassionate conservatism.

Egalitarianism was the one ideology that the absolute poverty concept was incompatible with. Logically, it was replaced with a concept that emphasized economic redistribution: in 1963, a new concept saw the light of day. Developed by Social Security Administration economist Mollie Orshansky,[14] the relative poverty concept defines a person as poor relative to the standard of living that other, better-off people enjoy.

President Johnson's working group that created the War on Poverty were quick to pick up on Orshansky's new, relative poverty concept. It is not clear whether their motivation was entirely ideological, or if it appealed to them because it removed the cap on government spending. The important effect of the concept was that people's status as entitled to government money now depended on a simple percentage number: if the income threshold for poverty is defined as 60 percent of median household income (the definition currently used by the European Union) then as median household income increases in actual dollars, so does the poverty threshold. As the poverty threshold rises, government must automatically spend more money on entitlements for the purposes of economic redistribution.

Relative poverty allows government to guarantee that the differences between the incomes of the poor and the incomes of others (or at least median-income households) will not change over time. This is the egalitarian essence in the relative definition of poverty.

By linking poverty to median income, President Johnson's Economic Opportunity Act marked the establishment of egalitarianism as the official ideology of the United States government. Since then, egalitarian thinking has guided the evolution of entitlement programs under the American welfare state. The food-stamp program is a good example. In 1964, when President Johnson signed the Food Stamp Act to make the program permanent, he also reconfigured the program so that its benefits would no longer be absolute. The basket of food that people could buy on food stamps evolved over time by means of the Cost of Living Adjustment (COLA) instrument, which protects the purchasing power of food stamps against inflation.

Because of annual COLAs, the food-stamp budget remains in constant relation to the standard that an average-income family enjoys. This keep-up-with-the-Joneses effect of the relative-poverty concept is reinforced by the income eligibility requirements of the program.

It has also been applied in entitlement programs created after the launch of the War on Poverty. Among those, the largest and probably best known program is the cash-redistributing Earned Income Tax Credit. Owing to its design, its entire purpose is to redistribute income; as it does, though, it also comes to represent one of the deeply rooted, inherent problems that burden the welfare state and, ultimately, pose a threat to its long-term survival.

The Earned Income Tax Credit

Simply put, the War on Poverty marked the start of the remaking of the United States from a free-market capitalist country to an egalitarian welfare state. It marked the phase-out of an era with strictly limited government, individual liberty, and unabridged property rights. In its place emerged an era where the balance between property rights and entitlements was reversed. Philosophically, the right of the entitled, which is tight under absolute poverty, becomes open-ended under relative poverty. The economic equivalent of this is a shift from natural limitations of government to an open-ended government spending commitment.

The philosophical shift manifests itself in a shift in the balance of rights between the taxpayer and the entitlement consumer. Under absolute poverty the taxpayer's right to keep his money supersedes the right of the entitled to receive entitlements. Under relative poverty the balance is altered, ranking the entitlement recipient's right to his money above the right of the taxpayer not to part with his money.

Egalitarianism is strongly reflected in the Earned Income Tax Credit (EITC), which is about a decade younger than Lyndon Johnson's War on Poverty. Created in the 1970s, it is clearly the product of the same egalitarian ideology as the War on Poverty: its benefits vary between eligible persons depending on their income and family size. Just like the relative-poverty concept, the EITC is redistributive both in theory and in practice. It also demonstrates how egalitarian thinking is not limited to entitlement programs, but also defines the design of the personal federal income tax system.

Over time, the EITC has become one of the most important entitlement programs in the federal budget. At $66.7 billion (2015), it costs almost as much as SNAP.[15] Its redistributive effects are clearly visible, with the benefits varying based on income and family size. The largest credit anyone can qualify for is $6,242 per year, but part of the real redistributive effect on people's income is in the amount of the credit relative to people's incomes.

In accordance with the purpose of income redistribution, the EITC gives more the less a person earns. Below is how the tax credit changes the income of a family of four, married, filing jointly.[16]

For the lowest income groups in Table 2.1, those making $20–$30,000 per year, the EITC is so big that they actually end up with more cash in their hand than their pre-tax income. For the upper-income groups, the EITC drops dramatically, leaving them with less money in their pockets than their pre-tax income.

TABLE 2.1 EITC impact

Income	*Income tax*	*Net income*	*EITC*	*Adj. Income*
$20,000	$2,081	$17,919	$5,348	$23,467
$25,000	$2,831	$22,169	$5,254	$27,423
$30,000	$3,581	$26,419	$4,201	$30,620
$35,000	$4,331	$30,669	$3,148	$33,817
$40,000	$5,081	$34,919	$2,095	$37,014
$45,000	$5,831	$39,169	$1,042	$40,211
$50,000	$6,581	$43,419	$0	$43,419

The EITC amplifies the redistribution effect already built into the federal personal income tax code. In 2013 households within the top 10 percent of incomes paid 69.8 percent of all personal federal income taxes.[17] At the other end of the income ladder, 28 million Americans shared the $67 billion given out by the EITC. As a result, they paid a minimum of federal income taxes, or none at all.[18] In fact, as Table 2.1 shows, the EITC turns some people into negative taxpayers as they get a bigger tax refund than the taxes they paid.

The sole purpose of the EITC is income redistribution, making it a perfect example of egalitarianism in practice. At the same time, it also represents one of the problems that are built into the welfare state and egalitarian political practice. Suppose the parent, in a family of four, earns $30,000 and is offered a promotion with a $5,000 raise. As Table 2.1 shows, his adjusted income, in other words income after federal income taxes and the EITC they qualify for, increases by $3,197. The tax effect, $1,803, is 36 percent.

All other things being equal, if this couple made twice as much and got a $5,000 raise, their marginal-income tax rate would only be 15 percent. To pay a marginal tax higher than 36 percent they would, by 2016 tax rates, have to make $467,000.

This effective marginal income tax is high enough to discourage many beneficiaries of the EITC from accepting a promotion or putting in extra hours at work. As more entitlement programs are added to the picture, the effective marginal tax rate rises rapidly, and with it, so does the threshold that discourages people from pursuing income-raising career moves.

Disincentives toward work-driven income improvements negatively affect labor supply, especially with higher skills and productivity. This uncontroversial fact should be open to discussion, not only among critics of the egalitarian project but first and foremost among its proponents and defenders. After all, a long-term trend of weak economic growth is like a slowly progressing venom to the welfare state; any factors that contribute to a slowdown in growth should be of great concern to all egalitarians.

That is not the case, though. On the contrary, disregard for the problems with slow economic growth is in fact widespread among the left. A good example is Senator Bernie Sanders, whose bid for the Democratic presidential ticket in 2016 catapulted him straight into the limelight of national politics. On more than one occasion he made himself the voice of the surprisingly well-received viewpoint that economic equality matters more than economic growth.

Egalitarians should think twice on this matter. Concern for economic growth is not just something that free-market economists like to talk about. As the next chapter explains, prominent economists whose contributions to the advancement of egalitarianism have gone down in history, were well aware that the egalitarian project – the welfare state – would not survive over time unless supported by strong economic growth.

Notes

1 Tanner and Hughes (2013).
2 Califano (1999).
3 Bartholomew (2016).
4 There are exceptions, of course. This is a general point aiming for the mainstream of conservative thinkers since the beginning of the War on Poverty.
5 Mitchell (1996).
6 Commager (1967).
7 Trattner (1999).
8 To an American audience, Gunnar Myrdal is probably best known for *An American Dilemma*. First published in 1944, this book discusses, in great detail, racial relations in early-twentieth-century America. It was so well received that it even came to influence the U.S. Supreme Court's famous *Brown v. Board of Education* case of 1954.
9 See www.lbjlibrary.org/press/civil-rights-tax-cuts-and-the-war-on-poverty (accessed May 18, 2017).
10 Bartholomew (2016).
11 Tanner and Hughes (2014).
12 In practice, absolute poverty concepts do change over time. However, those changes are neither automatic nor driven by annual increases in median household income or any other relative criteria. Instead, they change as a result of changes to the public perception of the difference between tolerable poverty and abject poverty.
13 Tanner (2007).
14 Fisher (1992). See also the Census Bureau's website page *Poverty – Experimental Measures*. Available at census.gov.
15 See www.eitc.irs.gov/EITC-Central/eitcstats?_ga=1.33397054.101481157.1474490063 (accessed May 18, 2017).
16 Internal Revenue Service, EITC Calculator and 1040 Tax Tables. It is assumed that the family has no deductions and no other income than from work.
17 See www.ntu.org/foundation/page/who-pays-income-taxes (accessed May 18, 2017).
18 Edwards and de Rugy (2015).

3

THE SWEDISH ROOTS OF THE AMERICAN WELFARE STATE

Economic redistribution is an established principle in American politics. There is plenty of evidence of this:

- Almost three quarters of the federal budget is directly or indirectly spent on economic redistribution;
- The federal income-tax system allows the lowest-earning 50 percent to pay 10 percent of the personal-income taxes while the highest-earning 10 percent pay 70 percent;
- The Reagan and Bush tax cuts, officially sold as supply-side policies for conservatives to support, in reality ended up raising more tax revenue to reinforce funding for the welfare state; and
- All entitlement programs from the War on Poverty and onward have been designed to put into practice the principle of economic redistribution.

It is, in other words, not an exaggeration to say that egalitarianism has conquered the federal budget. It has done so with undeniable bipartisan support, a fact that is startling both from an ideological viewpoint – the acceptance of egalitarianism de facto constitutes a conservative ideological surrender – and from an empirical perspective.

To the latter point, the pervasive presence of egalitarianism in government policies over the past several decades has had deep, lasting consequences for the American economy. At the forefront of those is a long-term decline in GDP growth, the cause of which is – at least in part – an unending expansion of entitlements and taxes for the purposes of economic redistribution. Figure 3.1 explains how economic growth suffers (right axis) and once entitlement spending exceeds 50 percent of the federal budget (left axis):

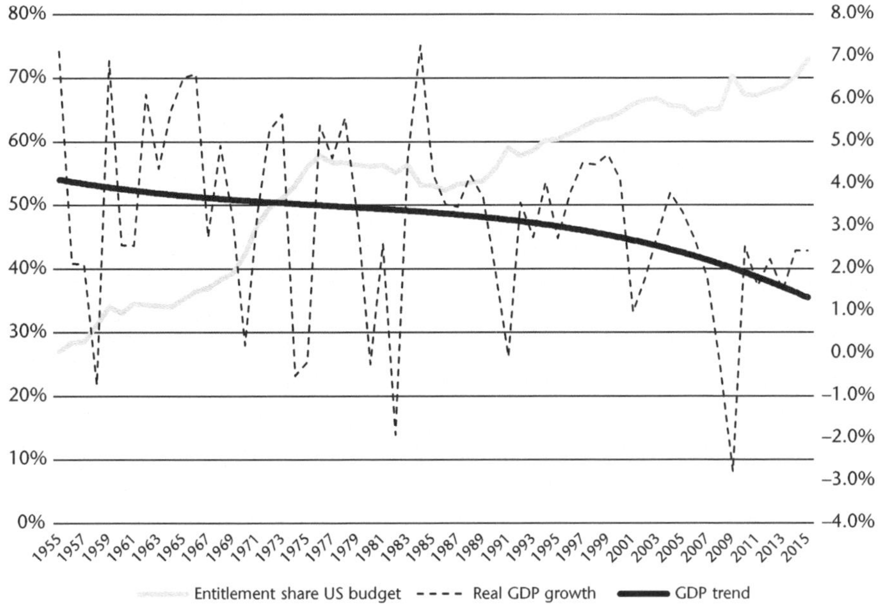

FIGURE 3.1 Real GDP growth: entitlement share of federal budget

Source: Office of Management and Budget; Bureau of Economic Analysis

While a correlation between two variables, as displayed here, is not in itself evidence of a causal relation, basic economic theory speaks in its favor. High taxes and generous redistributive entitlements with high marginal effects as in the Earned Income Tax Credit, together create an economic environment that discourages career development and entrepreneurship. Overall, the welfare state discourages reliance on one's own ability to provide a prosperous life for one's family.

The question, therefore, is not if there is a causal relationship from the growth of the American welfare state to the slowdown of GDP growth; the real question is why this slowdown has not attracted more attention than it has – especially among supporters of economic redistribution.

Logical or not, the answer is found in the deeper layers of egalitarian thinking. It starts with the premise that government is never big enough.

The unending pursuit of egalitarianism

Despite the facts that:

- the federal government spends \$2.7 trillion on economic redistribution;
- the states and local governments add almost \$1.3 trillion to that number;

- egalitarian programs in the federal budget outspend national defense by a factor of seven to one;

egalitarians still want more entitlement spending and thereby more economic redistribution. On their agenda for the future we find universal child care, general income security including tax-paid family leave for all, and single-payer health care.

The reasons for this unending pursuit of bigger government are found in the origins of the egalitarian project. Its first ideological elements were formulated in the early nineteenth century, but it was not until the 1920s and 1930s that some European governments tried to put the ideology into systematic political practice.

However, despite its profound economic and political impact, the practice of egalitarianism in America was only a follow-up on numerous European endeavors into the realm of economic redistribution. Among those, Sweden stands out as the cradle of egalitarianism. Its welfare state gained global recognition during the mid-twentieth century, lauded around the world as the epitome of egalitarian success. In fact, the ideological foundations of the modern welfare state were built in 1934 by two Swedes:

- Gunnar Myrdal, economist, founder of the Institute for International Economics in Stockholm and winner of the 1974 Nobel Memorial Prize in Economics (shared with F.A. Hayek); and
- His wife, Alva Myrdal, sociologist, member of the Swedish Parliament and Deputy Minister of Foreign Affairs in the Prime Minister's Cabinet; in 1982 she was awarded the Nobel Peace Prize for her involvement in the global disarmament movement.

They outlined their bold egalitarian vision in a very influential book. Its Swedish title, *Kris i befolkningsfrågan*, is best translated as *The Demographic Crisis*; it has never been officially translated into English. This is a pity, since the book outlines in crisp detail the ideological foundation for what soon became the role model for welfare states all around the world.

What really stood out with the Myrdals' book is how they were able to transform their ideological project into political and legislative practice. Their plan to remake Sweden from the ground up aimed at creating a society that had not just reduced, but *completely eliminated* income differences. No two individuals would enjoy different standards of living.

Their goal was a society where economic self-interest was eliminated from the plate of individual motivations. It was a society built on the principles of absolute egalitarianism.

It is important to understand the practical meaning of this ideology. It literally stipulates that nobody shall ever make more money than anybody else; nobody shall ever enjoy a higher standard of living than anybody else. A physician and a plumber; an aircraft engineer and a janitor; a math professor and a gas station attendant; all should earn the same amount of money and live on the same economic standard.

Literally, the same.

As founders of the Swedish welfare state, Mr. and Mrs. Myrdal inspired many followers around the world. One of them was John Kenneth Galbraith, a Harvard economist who was also one of the most influential policy advisors behind the War on Poverty. It was in good part thanks to his work that Lyndon Johnson's War on Poverty came to be influenced by not only the ideological foundation of the Swedish welfare state, but also its institutional practice.

The vision of absolute egalitarianism has not yet materialized in the United States, nor has it become a reality in Sweden. In fact, income differences persist around the world, even where welfare states have been up and running for decades. In his *Inequality and Instability*, James K Galbraith demonstrates in great detail, using a variety of quantitative methods, how economic differences prevail, both within countries and in international comparisons.[1] Critics of economic redistribution would use his findings to argue that the pursuit of the egalitarian goal is feeble, that the goal is unattainable and that the world has paid dearly for the egalitarian project.

Supporters of egalitarianism, on the other hand, would not see the not-yet-achieved goal as a problem; so long as the goal post has not been reached, the march continues toward it. In practice, this means steadfast expansion of the entitlement roster under the realm of the welfare state. According to egalitarian theory, every new entitlement program brings us a little bit closer to the elimination of economic differences. Until the goal of absolute egalitarianism has been reached, the argument is that there will always be a need for new entitlement programs.

Redistribution, growth and central economic planning

The harder egalitarians push for continuous expansion of government, the more pointed is the conflict between economic redistribution and economic growth. If current macroeconomic trends are not enough to convince egalitarians that this is a systemic problem built into the welfare state, then perhaps the founders of the welfare state can convince them. They predicted that growth was going to be a problem as government expanded, taxes went up and more and more money was spent on economic redistribution.

Foremost among the predictors of inadequate growth were actually Gunnar and Alva Myrdal. In their work to define the foundation of the Swedish welfare state, they spent a fair amount of time in their book *The Demographic Crisis* outlining policies to maximize economic growth. Regardless of the end results of the welfare state – which we can witness from the vantage point of the early twenty-first century – economist Gunnar Myrdal deserves recognition for having foreseen, in the early 1930s, that the welfare state would not survive without strong economic growth.

At the time the Myrdals published their book, in 1934, the world had limited experience of large, redistributive governments. The concept of economic re-distribution was not unknown – on the contrary, the philosophical roots of egalitarianism run all the way back to the early 1800s – but it had never before been applied to a society at the systemic level.[2] Therefore, the macroeconomic costs of big government were mostly theoretical at that point.

Despite the lack of evidence to support the concerns that a big welfare state would permanently slow down the economy, Gunnar Myrdal, already an accomplished economist at a young age, took the problems with slow growth seriously; he and his wife integrated the goal of strong growth into the goal formulation for welfare-state reforms. Unless economic growth could be kept at sufficiently high levels, the Myrdals were very concerned that the welfare state would not have the tax base needed for making absolute egalitarianism happen.

The benefits of growth are not really that complicated. Anyone who has ever shared a pizza with friends knows that ordering "extra large" instead of "medium" leaves everyone with bigger slices.

As the Myrdals and the Swedish Social Democrat Party went to work on creating the welfare state, they produced new entitlement reforms as if they were using a legislative assembly line. Starting in 1938, four years after the publication of *The Demographic Crisis*, the Social Democrats put the Myrdals' welfare-state vision into practice. Their reforms were carefully crafted, covering practically every aspect of life in Sweden: health care, child care, schools, income security, and so on.

With the same attention to detail, the Social Democrats also rolled out an economic-policy strategy for growth maximization. Known to economics-wonks as the Rehn-Meidner (RM) model, it has gone down in history as one of the most sophisticated attempts at central economic planning in a non-communist country.

The problem that the RM model was designed to solve started with the dilemma that the sustainable tax base needed by a welfare state was directly dependent on a sustainable private sector. Yet the very purpose of the welfare state was to fundamentally alter the conditions of the private sector's existence. To get around this dilemma, the RM model developed a policy strategy that would produce a maximum of tax revenue while guaranteeing competitive businesses access to strong markets with unrelenting demand for their products.

Both Gunnar Myrdal and the economists who gave name to the RM model, Gösta Rehn and Rudolf Meidner, understood that when taxes are imposed on a thriving economy, they gradually make the economy less able to thrive over time. They devised different strategies around this problem: Myrdal proposed massive public-sector investment programs, primarily in home construction; Rehn and Meidner followed another route. The key to a solution, they said, was for businesses to find a market for their products that was not tarnished by confiscatory Swedish taxes.

That market, said Rehn and Meidner, was global: the exports market, for short.

There was just one problem: the global market for just about any product is cut-throat competitive, saturated as it is with suppliers. Since Sweden at the time (the 1950s) was part of the Bretton Woods global exchange rate system, it could not use currency devaluations to give its businesses an edge on the global market. Instead, the RM model outlined a "third" path for economic policy.[3]

The first order of business was to make sure wages did not increase faster than businesses could afford while remaining globally competitive. In order to assure across-the-board restraint in wage growth, the RM model meant centrally negotiated wages. One national union cartel – known in Swedish as *Landsorganisationen* or by its acronym LO – represented all blue-collar workers in the country, while an equivalent organization spoke for all employers. Together they sat down in annual wage negotiations, resulting in a grand agreement applicable to the entire blue-collar labor market.

Later on, a similar wage-negotiation policy was put in place for wage agreements between the national union of white-collar professionals and the employers' organization. When that part had been added, centralized wage agreements would dictate wages and salaries in all industries.

It is, understandably, difficult for an American to grasp, or even find interest in, this wage-setting method. However, it is very important in the explanation of why the Swedish economy was able to thrive for decades, despite the rapid construction of the world's most sophisticated welfare state.

Sweden's centralized wage negotiations would best be "translated" to American conditions by putting AFL-CIO in the same room as the U.S. Chamber of Commerce. There, they would have complete authority to dictate wages and wage increases in every business in America. As crazy at it seems, this was nevertheless an essential part of the Swedish political strategy to build, and economically sustain, a full-scale welfare state.

Centralized wage negotiations began in 1938 with an accord between the national union cartel and the employers' federation. That accord would function as the guideline for wage setting in private businesses for about half a century. Its purpose was to keep labor costs below a certain benchmark and thereby allow exporting businesses to price their products competitively on the global market. As a result, sustained growth in exports would multiply throughout the rest of the economy and keep the tax base expanding at high rates.

Another part of the RM model's policy strategy to maximize growth in the tax base was fiscal and monetary policies that keep inflation at bay. On the fiscal side, that means balancing the government budget over a business cycle, that is, no accumulation of debt over time, while monetary policy is concentrated on keeping interest rates high. Constrained fiscal policy worked out well during the early decades of the welfare state's life, but as government grew it became increasingly difficult for government to restrain deficits.

With nationalized wage negotiations in place, and inflation under control, only one piece remained before the RM model had been put to full use. This part of the model aimed at maximizing productivity in the exports industry. High productivity helps a business keep prices down while also being able to reach big market volumes.

Here, the centralized wage negotiations once again played a crucial role. By making the national wage agreements applicable to all businesses in the country, the Swedish union cartel and the employer federation not only kept wages from rising above what the exporting corporations could pay, but they also kept them from falling too far below that level. Under the banner "solidarity in wages" the union cartel maintained, for decades, that wages across the labor market should be guided by, and dovetail, wages in businesses with most of their sales abroad. This led to a compressed wage structure that was beneficial to the large exporting corporations whose profits soared, but it also led to a cost squeeze on less productive, less profitable businesses.

This pressure was entirely intentional. Economists Rehn and Meidner suggested that "solidarity in wages" would weed out unprofitable businesses, reallocate capital and labor to the highly productive ones and thereby help keep profits up throughout the private sector.

When the private sector is dominated by large, highly profitable corporations, the welfare state has a big tax base to feed off. Figure 3.2 presents a simple schematic over the reasoning behind the RM model – the profitable companies benefit from "solidarity in wages" with very high profits, while other businesses are forced to shut down because they cannot pay the "solidarity" wage:

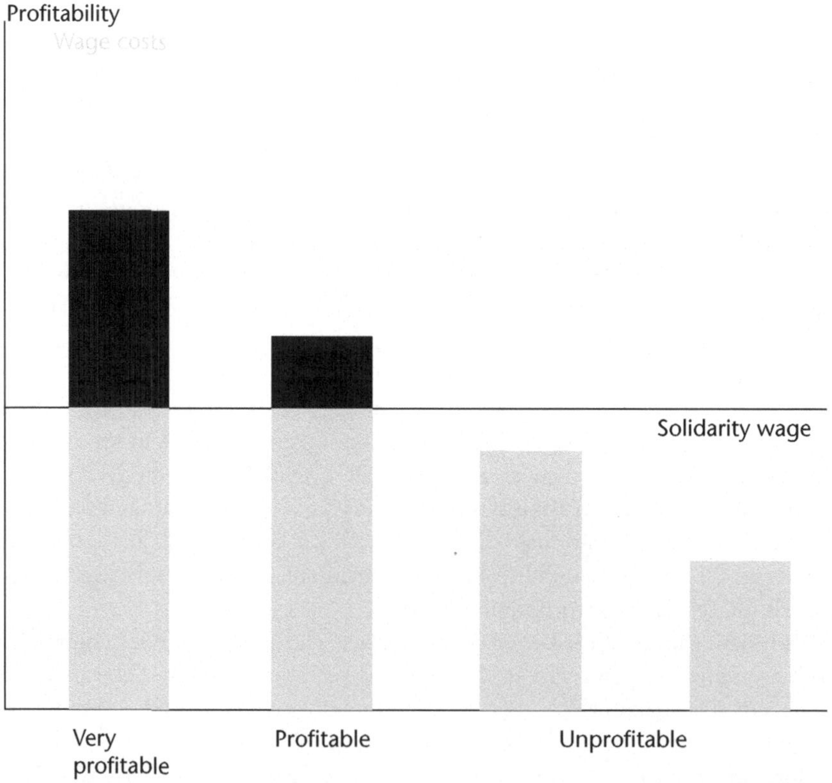

FIGURE 3.2 The RM model at work

Source: Office of Management and Budget; Bureau of Economic Analysis

The RM model turned out to be exactly what the Swedish welfare state needed. Evidence of its early success is in the growth rates for the Swedish economy: in the 1950s Swedish GDP matched the U.S. growth rate; in the 1960s Sweden nudged ahead, outgrowing the world's largest economy for most of the decade.

Just as predicted by the RM model, Sweden built many large, highly profitable multi-national businesses: Volvo, SAAB, Scania, Ericsson, ASEA (later ABB), Electrolux, Atlas Copco, Alfa Laval, IKEA. Backed by "solidarity in wages," which allowed them to pay their workers less than what the free market would otherwise have prescribed, these multi-national corporations had no problem paying the taxes that the welfare state needed – at least during the first 30 to 40 years of the welfare state.

They also benefited from a government that would basically do anything to keep them happy. In fact, the Swedish government practically created a central-planning program to combine its egalitarian policies with maximization of GDP growth. For example, starting already in the late 1930s it went out of its way to take control over all home construction in Sweden; there is no better example of the expansion of an egalitarian government into a private industry:

- Home standards were regulated by the national government as part of an entitlement-driven housing policy: as explained by the Myrdals in *The Demographic Crisis*, a family's personal finances should not prevent them from obtaining a certain housing standard.
- Owing to regulatory micro-managing of the housing market, government forced the costs of homes to rise; as a counter-measure, the Swedish parliament created housing subsidies for families defined as "low income".
- As a result of available housing subsidies, demand outpaced supply of homes compliant with government regulations; to increase home construction, government began issuing low-cost credit to expand home-construction financing.
- To further standardize home construction and thereby guarantee both compliance with regulations and low-cost production, the national Swedish government encouraged the formation of city-owned, non-profit corporations to build, own and maintain large subdivisions of apartment homes; already in the 1940s government had practically monopolized the stock and the production of apartment homes (with single-family living gradually dwindling to more or less a "luxury" for the upper-middle class).

By means of these steps, government could then use its master control over the housing market to provide for the needs of the nation's large, export-oriented conglomerates. Thanks to the "solidarity in wages" policies, it was difficult to the point of impossible for private businesses to thrive in Sweden's remote northern regions. Unemployment was curtailed by government migration policies, forcing those who filed for unemployment benefits to move south and take a job in a multi-national corporation. A combination of carrots in the form of "moving subsidies," and sticks in the form of unemployment-benefit cut-offs motivated countless families to leave Sweden's north for the sprawling cities in the south.

There was just one, obvious problem: housing. To solve the problem, the Social Democrat government launched a centrally planned home-construction program. Families moving from the north found new apartment homes, comfortably integrated into designed communities with shopping centers, schools, health clinics, libraries and mass transit.

These new communities were rolled out on an increasingly mass-production-like scale, not unlike what one could witness in the Soviet sphere of Europe during the Cold War.[4]

It was not just home construction that came under government planning. By the late 1960s, the Social Democrat government had coordinated all forms of economic policies into one centrally planned master strategy. Absolute egalitarianism was their driving philosophy; the welfare state was their way of turning that philosophy into legislative action; fiscal and monetary policy backed up government control over the labor market, housing, infrastructure, health care, education and welfare. All these policies were coordinated under the welfare state, as a means toward the egalitarian end.

As the welfare state came to its institutional completion in the late 1950s, Sweden effectively transformed itself from a market economy to a big government economy. The private sector was reduced to a support role for the welfare state.

Egalitarian conquest: Sweden and beyond

With the lightning-fast expansion of entitlements during the construction phase of the Swedish welfare state, it was easy for the Social Democrats to keep winning elections. From their victory in 1932 they were re-elected in 11 elections in a row. This is hardly surprising, given how the welfare state, in its early stage, seemed to give people something for nothing: health care, education, subsidized housing and general income security were paid for primarily with progressive income taxes. Those taxes, in turn, concentrated much of the tax burden onto high-income and high-wealth individuals, reinforcing the redistributive effect of the welfare state.

To large layers of the population it seemed as though the welfare state provided free goodies from government. A majority of the Swedish population believed it; the systemic problems with the welfare state did not begin to show up until the 1970s. In the meantime, egalitarianism spread throughout Europe, to a point where, today, it is woven into the European socio-economic fabric. With the exception of Margaret Thatcher's time as British prime minister, no conservative European politician has stood up to the expansion of government under the welfare state. On the contrary, egalitarianism has become inseparable from the European existence.

There are many reasons for the egalitarian triumph in Europe, some of which help explain its conquest of America. No country offers a more concentrated explanation of the welfare state's success than Sweden; the Swedish success of egalitarianism is particularly important to an American audience precisely because of the ideological kinship between the Swedish and American welfare states.

As mentioned, the Swedish welfare state's victory was due in part to the initially successful combination of entitlements, progressive taxes and the RM economic-policy model. Expectably, the perception of getting something for nothing could turn the most stalwart critic into an ardent supporter.

In addition to its initial economic strength, the welfare state benefited from consistent ideological back-up. Already in the 1950s, Swedish conservatives found themselves fighting an increasingly uphill battle of ideas against the rapidly expanding egalitarian project. They slowly retreated, gradually conceding defeat and accepting the egalitarian victory. In fact, in 1984, Gunnar Heckscher, renowned Swedish conservative politician, ambassador and former professor of political science, explained that the welfare state is a matter of fact, with its merits and its problems, regardless of what its critics may think.[5]

On this point, the United States is no different. Ever since the War on Poverty began, American conservatives have been on the defensive, gradually losing ground to egalitarians. Their retreat has been slower and less coordinated than in Europe, but it has nevertheless been a fact.

One important reason for the conservative retreat – which at least in the Swedish case is rightfully called a defeat – is that they, generally, have not spent nearly the time necessary to fully understand their ideological adversary. In the Swedish case, it was not until Heckscher's book in 1984 that the conservative movement had begun fully grasping the full scale of the egalitarian project; in the United States, conservatives are still generally torn between comprehending and resisting a welfare state, the full nature of which they still have not grasped. Among the many components of the egalitarian project, the conservative lack of attention to the relative poverty concept stands out as perhaps most damning. There is practically no discussion among conservatives on this matter; by default, the relative concept has won, whereupon the ideological core of economic redistribution has come to stand unchallenged.

By failing to study the ideological depths of egalitarianism, conservatives have missed out on a chance to launch an ideological counterstrike against the welfare state. There are big wins waiting for conservatives in tracing the idea of income redistribution back to the inherently authoritarian origins of egalitarianism.

A conservative ideological counterstrike would have to begin with the tracing of the roots of American egalitarianism further back in time than the War on Poverty. While the thinkers behind President Johnson's signature accomplishment were all brilliant in their own right, the foremost among them, John K Galbraith, was heavily influenced by Swedish egalitarian thought. At the time of his contributions to President Johnson's administration, the Swedish welfare state had been fully developed and was in the prime of its macroeconomic success. It was hardly surprising that Galbraith would draw inspiration from a welfare state that seemed to have such an impressive track record as the Swedish one had in the late 1950s and early 1960s.

Since the Myrdals' book *The Demographic Crisis* formulated the ideological foundation of the welfare state, a quest to unravel its ideological core must begin with a careful examination of their work. This book, basically a manual for turning egalitarian ideology into legislative practice, centers in on two ideas:

1 Absolute egalitarianism – meaning:
   a The complete elimination of economic differences between citizens; and
   b The removal of restrictions on the size of government.
2 Ideological ends justify political means – meaning:
   c Government management of the population stock;
   d Subordination of the individual to the collective; and
   e Redefinition of the family.

The meaning of "absolute egalitarianism" is already clear: the complete elimination of income differences between individual citizens. Taken literally, as it should, it calls for government intervention into the economy until no one citizen's life is economically different than the economic life of another. Regardless of what Jack and Jill do for a living, under absolute egalitarianism their incomes, their consumption and their opportunities to advance economically are identical.

Theoretically, the concept of absolute egalitarianism is simple to understand. It is perhaps more difficult to grasp the practical meaning of this concept, namely the removal of any restrictions on government involvement in our lives.

Practical egalitarianism begins with the recognition that the ideological ends justify the political means. No expansion of government is ruled out if it helps advance egalitarianism. Among the means that government has at its disposal is the so called "population stock." The Myrdals pepper this term throughout their book, and it means exactly what it sounds like. It refers to the entire population of a country as a herd of cattle; an instrument for economic policy; a tool for social transformation.

The term is essential to the advancement of egalitarianism and its construction of the welfare state. In order to eradicate economic differences between individuals, say the Myrdals, government needs to transform the "population stock." It is important to remember that this is about the advancement of absolute egalitarianism, which again leads to the complete elimination of any economic differences between individual citizens.[6]

The question, then, is what exactly the Myrdals had in mind when they said that the welfare state needs a new, demographically planned population stock. After all, the idea of transformation or planning in any demographic context bears an uncomfortable resemblance to the Nazi experiments with eugenics in 1930s Germany, does it not?

Yes, it does. To say that government should engage in demographic planning is to say that government should reconfigure its population in compliance with some standard set by political ideologues. In the case of Nazi Germany the goal was to purify the German race, but also to breed a viable population strong enough –

according to Nazi definitions – to be productive and raise a new generation of ideologically even more "approvable" Germans.

In their book *The Demographic Crisis*, the Myrdals excluded the racial component of demographic planning, but otherwise the purpose they gave for transforming the Swedish population was eerily similar to what the Nazis said they wanted for the Germans. As the Myrdals saw it, the Swedish population of the early 1930s (when they wrote their book) was not strong enough, physically or mentally, to build, let alone sustain a society without economic differences. As they saw it, absolute egalitarianism requires perennially high economic growth, which can only be accomplished if the population is strong enough and can function as a highly productive workforce.

However, as the Myrdals made abundantly clear throughout their book, demographic planning also means "weeding out" individuals who will cost the welfare state more over their lifetime than they will contribute to it in the form of taxes. This part of their demographic planning idea is rarely if ever mentioned in the debate over the welfare state, yet it has an economic meaning that is just as important to the advancement of the egalitarian welfare state as is the need for a productive workforce. That economic meaning can be translated into a simple government budget equation:

- A welfare state cannot live above its means, especially not long-term.
- By maximizing the physical and mental strength of the population, the Myrdals sought to maximize labor productivity.
- High rates of labor productivity lead to high rates of GDP growth and, consequently, high levels of tax revenue.
- By minimizing the physical and mental "deficiencies" of the population, the Myrdals sought to minimize the costs of entitlement programs and, consequently, secure the fiscal sustainability of the welfare state.

This is where demographic planning, or transformation of the population, or eugenics, becomes essential to the long-term survival of the welfare state. As part of a strategy to keep the costs down for the welfare state's entitlement programs, the Myrdals wanted to "radically sift out individuals that are highly unfit to live" (p. 217).

The idea of "sifting out" individuals is every bit as blunt and brutal as it sounds. At the same time, it is important to note that their preferred instruments for practicing eugenics did not reach the atrocious levels of the Nazi version of demographic planning. The Myrdals confined themselves to forced sterilization in order to "sift out" the "highly unfit."

When only the "approved" part of the population reproduces, its total ability to produce tax revenue for the welfare state is radically enhanced. At the same time, its cost to the welfare state in terms of health and mental care is minimized.

To drive home their point about the "need" to transform the "population stock," the Myrdals devote a ten-page long section in Chapter 7 of their book to the idea of sterilizing the "highly unfit" by force. It is put in the context of something called "prophylactic social policy," which the Myrdals discuss in the opening of Chapter 7 of *The Demographic Crisis:*[7]

> The direct purpose of the prophylactic social policy is to produce a better human stock. The quality aspect [of the population] rises in importance already because the population is stagnant and then declines at an accelerating rate. So long as the population is growing at high rates the quality aspect is easily reduced to insignificance. At that point it presents itself immediately to view the human stock as merely fuel for industrial production, the use of which does not have to be guided by frugality, as it is supplied in such abundance; "cannon fodder". However, when the demographic stock responds to its living conditions by ceasing to reproduce itself, one is inclined to carefully address the question to what extent these living conditions could be the result of the quality of the demographic stock itself, and to what extent that stock can be improved upon.

In other words, it is of utmost importance for the welfare state to have a steadily rising flow of tax revenue to rely on. In order to secure that steady increase, government must "guarantee" steady economic growth. It is a necessary condition for steady economic growth, in turn, that the supply of labor is of the highest possible quality.

Securing the genetic standard of the population by "sifting out" the "highly unfit" is only the first step of egalitarian demographic planning. To maximize the economic resources available to the welfare state, the Myrdals suggest as a second step that government plan and configure the nation's labor supply. Once sterilization has maximized the genetic potential for high productivity among the population, it is time for government to hone the skills and attitudes of the future workforce.

Put plainly: government-run education.

Publicly funded and operated schools did not come about with the welfare state. The history of public education goes far back in time. In fact, public education is so widely accepted today that we never think of it as an entitlement, even though that is precisely what it is. Government pays for it through taxes that are collected independently of how many children the individual taxpayer sends to school. On the other side of the equation, education is provided independently of the individual family's ability to pay the cost of their children's education.

In other words, public education is an entitlement that functions as an instrument for economic redistribution. That, however, does not mean that it is incompatible with a non-egalitarian society. Public education has a history in America that is as long as that of the first colonies. In its early days, the Commonwealth of Massachusetts passed the "Great Deluder Act" to provide public education on Christian values to all children, and to teach them reading, writing and other basic skills so they would not be deluded into destructive, anti-social behavior by "the great deluder" himself.

Thomas Jefferson expanded on the idea of public education. He wanted all young Americans to be educated enough so that they could inherit, and be the stewards of, the free and prosperous country where they had grown up.

Because of the long history of public education in the United States, we do not necessarily think there is anything wrong with it in general, especially if it provides a pathway to a better life for children of poor families. However, egalitarians do not see education quite the same way. To the founders of the Swedish welfare state, the main purpose of education was to prepare the growing generation for productive workforce participation where every individual is steered by the education system toward an occupation where, according to the same education system, that individual will be most productive.

Prophylactic social policy

In a comparison between the egalitarian project as outlined by the Myrdals and egalitarians in the twenty-first century, one is struck by the strong emphasis on economic growth and macroeconomic performance in the vision of the Myrdals. This element of economic thinking is almost entirely absent among modern proponents of the welfare state; if they make any such references, it is to suggest that egalitarianism in itself is good for economic growth.

According to the Myrdals, it was absolutely essential to secure perennially high rates of GDP growth. Their repeated references to "prophylactic social policy" and demographic planning exemplify their deep concerns that the welfare state not be structurally under-funded. Their education policies are also configured largely to secure the fiscal sustainability of the welfare state. This is done in part through the maximization of workforce preparation by means of K-12 education.

In order to do so, the Myrdals do not want to spread taxpayers' resources too thin. One of the problems for the poor, they say, is that they have too many children. People in poverty, they say, have more children than they can care for, either because they do not understand better or because they think many children means a greater chance that someone will take care of them when they grow old.

This problem, the Myrdals said, is best solved by means of income redistribution.

In Chapter 7 of *The Demographic Crisis* the Myrdals outline a reform agenda aimed at conforming living conditions for families with young children. They firmly believe that income redistribution weakens the reproductive urge among the poor. But they also believe that poor parents are unable to provide for the proper upbringing of their own children. Therefore, society as a whole – represented by government – needs to step in and correct for poor people's ineptitude in bringing up their own children (p. 205):

> The direct purpose of prophylactic social policy is to bring forward a better human material.

And, on page 11 (emphasis added):

> It will be a question of fairly radical redistribution of income between families with different support burdens in terms of numbers of children and with different incomes. It will be a matter of a *prophylactic social policy*, primarily governed by the purpose of *raising the quality of the demographic stock* while at the same time realizing the radical redistribution policy by means of socializing the better part of the cost for raising children.

In other words, it takes a village to raise a child.

This idea is not unique to the Myrdals. It has been a lead motive of egalitarian thinking since at least the socialist utopians of the early 1800s. Swedish historian Yvonne Hirdman puts the utopians' instrumental view of children in the context of modern-day Swedish welfare-state policies:[8]

> The utopian idea of happiness was intimately connected with the place, needs and tasks of women in the "new society." The "woman question" was a fundamental issue in the utopian blueprints of Robert Owen and Charles Fourier, the two most important creators of early nineteenth-century utopias. For example, Fourier thought of sexual love as one of the most important relations among members of his imagined harmony. Living in big, Versailles-like houses called the Phalangsthere, the inhabitants of his utopia would all have the opportunities of acting, working and being creative ... Children would be taken care of by the "community" and be reared in the utmost freedom, where their talents would be explored and developed. Owen ... also imagined the women of his utopia as free, with access to work, to politics, to love and with freedom from children as well. Children, for both of these thinkers, were a kind of raw material for making the "new man," the smallest unit of the "new society."

When prophylactic social policy leads to lower birth rates, the Myrdals explain, the need for public education as part of demographic planning increases. When fewer children are born into each new generation, government wants to make sure that every individual child is of the highest genetic quality with the highest possible social and economic potential. Demographic planning thus aims for an enhanced population stock, able to maximize economic output and to minimize the burden that "highly unfit" individuals impose on society.

From words to action: the uniform education system

Thanks in part to their book, the Myrdals gained significant influence over the Swedish Social Democrat government's policies from the late 1930s onward. Gunnar Myrdal served as a member of parliament and later secretary of trade, which no doubt helped him and his wife put their brand on the Social Democrat government's policies.

The construction of the Swedish welfare state followed two tracks, faithfully putting the Myrdals' ideas to work. The first track, aimed at increasing, and perpetuating, economic growth, had three major components: education reform, housing construction policies and labor market policies.

Reforms to the education system aimed at conforming and centralizing elementary and secondary education. (Later on the Social Democrats took it upon themselves to make similar reforms to the country's colleges and universities.) In 1940, the Social Democrat government began creating a national, centrally governed and funded, unitary school system. Starting in 1949 they gradually transferred control over the education system from local jurisdictions to the national government. A national school curriculum became reality in 1955, with a major revision in 1968.

The nationalization of the Swedish education system was driven by the economic considerations behind the welfare state. As the Myrdals spelled out, large, expensive entitlement programs required massive tax revenue; to maximize tax revenue they recommended policies for perennially strong economic growth. This need for growth guided the institutional changes during the two-decades long reform of the Swedish education system.

Education reforms can, in theory, improve GDP growth if they improve the quality of the nation's workforce. In order to maximize the economic output from the training of the workforce, the education system must guide students in order to:

a) Maximize their productivity once they join the workforce; and
b) Minimize the "waste" in the form of non-productive individual educational choices.

The nationalization of the education system is a first step in this direction, with curricular centralization as a second step. By nationalizing the system, funding is automatically conformed as a one-size-fits-all model. This will, again in theory, guarantee that all schools provide education of similar quality.

By centralizing the curriculum, government defines the educational paths that students can take. Given the goal of growth maximization, the public school system will offer students educational choices that will maximize the likelihood of them getting a job after school, and being productive in that job. The flip side of this system is that little if any resources are invested in courses and programs that fill no obvious productive purpose.

Educational reforms that nationalize and centralize the school system automatically end local influence and minimize individual student choice. The student enters an educational apparatus the purpose of which is to transform him or her into a productive member of the workforce and proud taxpayer.

This, however, makes the school reform a tough sell to parents and others who prefer local control, local financing and more opportunities for the student. Few if any parents genuinely want fewer choices and more centralized control over their children's education. Therefore, the egalitarian project adds a sales pitch to its educational reform package: education is no longer a civic responsibility as it was when the institution of the public school was first created; instead, it is an entitlement, a "social right of citizenship."

Hrovje Kap, sociologist and an expert on Swedish education reform, demonstrates how this ideological line of thinking was turned into practice as the school system underwent an egalitarian transformation. Schools were institutionally integrated and students subjected to "curricular streaming," essentially meaning that they were all placed in the same level of academic ability. Methods for differentiating students based on academic skills and performance were delayed until higher levels, giving preference to egalitarian goals in education. However, the reforms were not sold as egalitarian, but as opening "equal opportunity" for all children. Kap explains (2009, p. 12):[9]

> The idea of an *enhetsskola* [uniform school] that is one school within one common institution for all pupils … was in the initial government bill of 1950:70,[10] which laid down the early general principles for this reform, aimed at enabling every Swedish youth to develop his or her abilities for future tasks in society, irrespective of social background.

In the egalitarian narrative, "educational opportunity" becomes "equality of opportunity." A uniform school system with "curricular streaming" is preferable to a diverse, liberal-arts oriented system. It is a system defined by limited student choice under a standardized, national school system. These choices are then designed primarily to maximize students' vocational and professional opportunities. The needs of the labor market *as determined by government* influence the design of the opportunities students have to form their own education within the nationalized, centralized uniform school system.

In addition to controlling the institutional structure of the education system, government also has the means, through a centralized curriculum, to inject ideologically relevant values into the school system. While many critics of the Swedish education reforms of the 1950s, 1960s and later have suggested that ideology played an increasing role in curricula, this issue is of less relevance in the context of the welfare state than the institutional changes themselves. However, for Americans who are interested in the potential for ideological contamination of a school system, the debate over the Common Core reform under President Obama may be of interest.

Thanks to the institutional reforms of the Swedish education system, the idea of liberal arts, the development of classical citizenship and the pursuit of scholarship for its own sake gradually vanished from the scene. When I went through the Swedish K-12 system in the 1970s and early 1980s, students were streamed – as Kap so aptly explains it – into making a choice between academic and vocational emphasis already for seventh grade. Those who made vocational choices almost invariably ended up choosing strictly vocational training programs after ninth grade. (Swedish high schools, covering grades 9 to 12, are approximate to American senior-high school.) After a two-year program they could be welders, auto mechanics, construction workers, painters or electricians. These programs did not provide basic preparedness for college, making sure that the vocational choice at seventh grade had lifelong repercussions.

By contrast, those who chose an academic emphasis were streamed toward professional choices in high school: you could choose from the pre-engineering program which almost always led students to a civil engineering degree; a sciences program from which many students continued with pre-med and medical school, or other college science degrees; an "economic" program emphasizing business administration, accounting, marketing and elementary finance; or a humanities program where students were heavily schooled in foreign languages.

None of these programs bore any similarity to the American liberal-arts tradition, where students are educated broadly and thereby offered a high degree of independence over their future. By streaming students into vocational or professional programs, the Swedish school system instead served the purpose of the welfare state as defined by Gunnar and Alva Myrdal: a labor force educated and tuned to the needs of a labor market where they would be highly productive and deliver a maximum of tax revenue to the welfare state.

Subsequently, the Swedish government has made some token reforms to the school system with a limited form of voucher-based private school choice. Curriculum-wise, and institutionally, the national government has maintained tight control and oversight over the system, thus limiting the ability of private education providers to offer the depth of school choice that is available in other countries with a high degree of educational freedom. Tight government oversight is superficially motivated by the fact that government still funds schools and a certain share of each intake of students must be prepared for college. However, other countries have managed to combine educational freedom with a tax-based funding model. Denmark is the primary example, but the home-schooling model and the freedom outside of the public education system in the United States also offers opportunities that are nowhere to be found in Sweden.

In other words, underneath the token reforms of school choice, the Swedish education system remains an integrated part of the welfare state. As such, it still serves its original purpose as outlined by the Myrdals some 80 years ago. Its institutional purpose is still to mold the growing generation into a productive workforce. Even though brave entrepreneurs and well-intended enthusiasts have tried to introduce a wider range of school choice than the national regulations allow, the egalitarian ideology that once guided the nationalization and centralization of the school system has survived and remains largely intact.

From words to action: single-payer health care

No welfare state is complete without a universal, single-payer health-care system; some proponents of a complete government takeover of the health insurance and health-care system consider it the epitome of moral compassion. Others, the Myrdals included, view socialized health care as an enhancement of efficiency in the provision of medical treatment and preventative care. In Chapter 7 of *The Demographic Crisis*, a chapter titled "Social Policy and the Quality of the Population," the Myrdals make clear their reasons for proposing a single-payer health-care system. They view as inevitable the continuous movement toward complete government control, funding and operation of the health-care system. But even more so, this transition into socialized health care – a term they have no problem using – is viewed as "the most important social policy reform with a prophylactic, quality-improving purpose" (pp. 238–239). "Society" they say, "must increasingly assume responsibility for the cure and prevention of diseases" (p. 239). They also go into detail as to how they would like to see the health-care system organized (p. 240):

> The construction of a system of well equipped, enthusiastically managed, government health clinics is the natural continuation of our successfully started work toward the improvement and socialization of the health-care system. In the future, these clinics must become the normal source of health inquiries from the public regarding medical conditions.

Overarching the details in their reform proposal, the Myrdals' purpose with socializing the Swedish health-care system was the same as with their education reforms. They wanted to maximize the productivity of the workforce, in this case by minimizing sick days and debilitating medical conditions. They were thoroughly convinced that there was no other way to achieve this than to have government take over the entire health-insurance and health-care system. In fact, they were so convinced of the supreme performance of a single-payer, government-run health-care system that they dismissed, in a ridiculing tone, privately practicing physicians as part of an erstwhile, outdated model for providing health care.

There is no mistaking the confidence of the Myrdals in government's ability to run an entire health-care system. History, however, has not been kind to the idea: single-payer systems are universally inferior at providing health care, both in a timely manner and at acceptable quality levels. In fairness, the Myrdals did not have access to the evidence available today, but that does not mean they were left in the dark as to the serious problems associated with government-run health care.

Britain introduced a national, mandatory health-insurance model already in 1911. A decade later the debate was flying high over whether or not the first ten years merited a continuation of the system, or if it should be dismantled and the country return to a market-based model instead. The interest from both sides in the British system was so intense that, for example, in 1920 the *Monthly Labor Review*, a publication of the Bureau of Labor Statistics at the U.S. Department of Labor, published a long analysis of the National Health Insurance Act of 1911.[11] The same journal published another article on the same subject in 1934.[12]

Even if the Myrdals did not have access to the American literature on the British health-care system, it would seem reasonable that they had invested some time in examining the British experience through literature from closer sources. The *British Medical Journal* paid a fair amount of attention to the government-run health-insurance system, in part as a reflection over whether the United States should copy the British model. Medical practitioners also participated in the debate, in part because their first-hand experience with the system was far from as positive as proponents often suggest. In fact, even physicians in favor of a government-run health system readily admitted that the British experience was checkered at best. As an example, in a 1921 article for the Supplement to the *British Medical Journal*, a physician, offering a passionate defense of the National Health Insurance system, raised the question whether or not the entire system should be abolished. Describing it as "a costly piece of machinery" he noted that the system was a burden on taxpayers, with the cost continuing to rise:[13]

> for the contributions both of employer and insured person have had to be increased, like nearly every other charge, and this at a time of great difficulty for the employer and of falling wages for the workman.

Facing little or no resistance, the Myrdals ignored the growing international body of debate over single-payer health care and forged ahead. Facts were not going to get in the way of the prime directive behind their political agenda, namely the complete elimination of income differences.

As their socialization plans began to translate into legislation, one of the first sacrifices was privately funded health care. Entirely in accordance with their derogatory attitude toward private health care, they saw it as critical to force medical professionals into the ranks of a single-payer system.

However, the ambition to abolish private health care was also driven by an ambition to reshape the attitudes of the general public. When people are used to being able to choose their own doctor, to pay him or her cash or with an insurance of their choice and when they are used to being able to see a specialist on an as-needed basis, they tend to harbor feelings of being free and independent. When, on the other hand, government is in control of something as personal as health care, they have no choice but to trust government with – literally – their life.[14]

The socialization of Swedish health care did not happen overnight: in a recent report for the Swedish Association of Regional and Local Governments, French political scientist Bruno Palier of the Centre National de la Recherche Scientifique points to a decades-long struggle where government relentlessly pushed the envelope in its desired direction, gradually breaking down its opposition. Among the foremost opponents were the country's physicians, though they were unable to hold out as the transition from private health insurance to a single-payer system gradually amassed more and more control in the hands of government. This inevitably meant the effective termination of private practice of medicine. Palier notes (2006, p. 15; my translation from Swedish):

> The gradual transition into government control took place by means of a phase-out of privately practicing physicians from government-controlled health care (especially hospitals) and through growing spending and expanded responsibilities for regional governments.

In 1948 a commission under the Swedish parliament, the Riksdag, proposed that the country go all the way to a single-payer health-care system. Over the next decade, step-by-step reforms gradually eliminated private compensation of medical practitioners. By the end of the 1950s it was no longer possible for general practitioners and most physicians in specialty practice, to provide health care on private funding. By the end of the 1960s all specialized health care, including elderly care, maternity care and psychiatry, had been incorporated under the single-payer system. And Sweden passed a milestone on the way to absolute egalitarianism.

From words to action: socialized housing

In its practice, the welfare state is essentially a master-planned effort at social engineering. When, as in the case with the Myrdals, these engineering ambitions include the entire population, they also reach into all corners and crevices of people's lives. The egalitarian transformation that began with children's educational experience and then completely revamped people's health care moves on to its next – but not last – target.

People's homes and communities

Few if any democratic countries have attempted to micro-plan the lives of their citizens to the extent that Sweden has done. As soon as the Social Democrat government started building the welfare state, it also engaged in detailed community and city planning. For both purposes, it went to great lengths to socialize the construction and ownership of people's homes.

During the late 1930s Swedish cities created their own housing corporations. As per the ideological directives of the Social Democrat government, these corporations were non-profit in nature. By constructing, owning and maintaining entire apartment complexes, they reshaped their cities and, thanks to a combination of tax subsidies and political bias, soon came to dominate the housing industry.

Called "public-purpose" corporations, these government-owned housing conglomerates brought to life a deeply held egalitarian idea, namely to build new homes designed in compliance with ideological desires. The Myrdals, whose influence in this area was as strong as in education and health care, were the boldest advocates of socially engineered housing, but they were not the first. Ideas of engineered communities have been around for a long time, often with focus on sharing resources and cohabitating on elaborate collectivist premises. However, before the Soviet empire and the Swedish welfare state, such ideas were micro-social and microeconomic in nature. They were confined to communities where the initiative belonged to a small group of dedicated founders and followers.

In the Soviet Union, central economic planning took a dictatorial form, just like the rest of the government system. The Swedish welfare state implemented a less authoritarian kind of planning, such as with the creation of public-purpose housing corporations. Those corporations replaced private competitors not by coercion, but by means of market-distorting policies. Foremost among those policies was a very generous funding model; the national government effectively gave the public-purpose corporations monopoly over apartment-based living in Swedish cities.[15]

Thanks to the government's emphasis on ideologically driven housing, Swedes live in apartments to a much larger extent than Americans. By de facto socializing the housing industry, the Social Democrats had at their disposal the housing policies they needed to take egalitarian social engineering to the micro level of people's lives.

On the one hand, for many families this meant a step up in terms of home standards, with modern appliances, indoor plumbing and well working heating and electricity supply. On the other hand, the government-funded, government-run home construction policies led to a high level of standardization – or conformity – in terms of home layout.

Not surprising, the dominance of the public-purpose corporations made it easy for government to pass and implement legislation on national home standards. In 1947 Sweden got its first national law standardizing the architecture of homes and their subdivisions. By law, in urban areas a family of four could live in a two-bedroom apartment. Also by law, the subdivision where they lived was configured for mass transit, not private car ownership.

To Swedes, living in a single-family home of the kind that is so common in the United States, has always been considered a dividing line between social classes. The public-purpose corporations and the strict housing regulations that came with the welfare state have for the most part perpetuated that dividing line. The egalitarian purpose behind the socialization of the housing industry never succeeded in eradicating the single-family home as an option for better-off families. Despite valiant attempts from the late 1930s well into the 1970s, the Social Democrats finally had to give up their most fervent egalitarian housing ambitions. The single-family home prevailed in a tarnished existence, but was associated in the public discourse with a privileged, upper-class lifestyle.

To this date, studies of all kinds of social issues in Sweden divide the population based on what type of home they live or grew up in. This is common practice in research on children's school performance, where children from single-family homes are often said to perform better than children who live in apartment complexes.

Despite ideologically charged efforts to stigmatize home ownership and single-family living, the Swedish housing market has slowly changed for the better since the 1980s. Today, slightly more than half of all Swedes live in single-family homes, though in actual numbers apartment homes still dominate the housing market.

The government-driven efforts to eradicate single-family living lost steam in the 1970s. It was, simply, far too expensive to continue its social-engineering housing efforts. A good part of the reason for this was embedded in the egalitarian ambitions behind socialized housing. As is often the case with government incursions into the free market, the regulatory efforts on the Swedish housing market created the need for more incursions.

The housing-standards regulations that began in the 1930s and became national law in 1947 regulated how apartment homes should be configured. There were two purposes behind this: to standardize home construction and thereby bring down costs; and to elevate the standard of living for a majority of the population. The problem was that the balance between these two purposes did not favor cost reduction – it ended up making home construction costlier on a per-unit basis (compared to how apartment homes had been configured and constructed up until the mid-1930s). The point behind regulating the very standard of apartments themselves was to put the vast majority of the population in homes better than what they were used to. Needless to say, the rising cost of per-unit construction made it increasingly difficult for families on low and moderate incomes to move in to government's newly constructed homes.

In other words, the very policies that were aimed at raising the housing standard for a majority of the population made it prohibitively expensive for them to take advantage of the higher standard.

This problem did not escape the Social Democrat government. However, instead of reverting to free-market conditions, they added a new law that capped the lease of an apartment owned and operated by the public-purpose companies to 20 percent of household income. The theory was that this would open housing, compliant with egalitarian ideological principles, to working-class families.

Government, however, missed out on one detail in their calculations, namely that their own regulations increased housing construction costs. Overlooking this detail, the Social Democrat government still ended up pushing apartment lease costs above one fifth of the income for most people who moved into government housing.

This time, the fix was not a new regulation, but a new entitlement program. The Swedish government created a housing subsidy specifically for low-income families.

When not even that helped, they came up with yet another subsidy, this time for the construction of homes that complied with the government's ideological ambitions. Builders could still go ahead with whatever homes they wanted to build, but the taxpayer-funded construction subsidies made such a big difference that much of the Swedish housing stock soon complied with egalitarian ideology.

However, the socialized housing policy still had not expanded far enough. The Social Democrats also wanted government housing to become a tool for quelling business cycle fluctuations that, according to Gunnar Myrdal and many other left-leaning economists, were caused by the free-market economy.

In fact, the belief that the business cycle is exclusive to free-market capitalism goes back to at least Karl Marx and his *Capital*. Like Marx, Gunnar Myrdal viewed the business cycle as an inherent weakness of free-market capitalism. Countless socialist economists, from Marx onward, have been firmly convinced that they can devise economic policies that would eliminate the business cycle altogether. Little do they understand that the business cycle is actually a sign of a healthy economy: the peaks of the cycle come about because entrepreneurs, consumers and investors are optimistic about the future; recessions happen because entrepreneurs, consumers and investors shift their mood from optimism to pessimism. This keeps them from making excessively foolish investments and taking severe risks. Recessions weed out unproductive businesses and free up resources to be used in more productive, more profitable business endeavors when the economy turns upward again.

Socialists believe that without the business cycle we would have perennially full employment. The Myrdals firmly made this argument in *The Demographic Crisis*: with the proper fiscal tools, they said, government could create perennially high GDP growth, maintain full employment – and generate enough tax revenue to fund even the most ambitious welfare state.[16]

However, this belief is based on the false notion that even if you somehow could eliminate the business cycle, it would be frozen in full-employment mode. There is no guarantee that this would be the case. Quite the contrary, actually, it is more likely that the measures of central economic planning needed to eliminate the business cycle would have a combined effect on the economy that would be strong enough to perpetuate under-utilization of labor and capital. Central economic planning, again the only way to break the business cycle, simply cannot replace the free market as the resource allocator. Everywhere it has been tried, the outcome has been a mix of economic stagnation and the death of entrepreneurship – either because it is banned legally or because it is discouraged by the stagnant economy.

These simple, indisputable facts made no difference to the Swedish Social Democrats who were determined to politicize – or ideologize – the home of every Swedish family. They adopted the Myrdals' idea that it was possible to use housing policies to kill the business cycle. On top of other policy instruments, such as housing subsidies to tenants, they radically expanded the supply of very favorable credits to construction companies. These credits, backed by the coercive force of taxation, undercut private competition to the point where government became the absolutely dominant provider of construction funding. Once in that position, government could use those credits as an instrument to keep construction activity up at all times.

From an egalitarian perspective, the elimination of the business cycle would provide a maximum of tax revenue for the welfare state. Furthermore, the expansion of the government's construction credits squarely benefited the government-owned public-purpose corporations, and thus they were able to effectively eliminate for-profit competition in housing construction. This ideologically desirable outcome transformed the entire industrial chain, from financing to construction to owning to maintaining apartment buildings. (The single-family home market was left largely untouched by government but also became much less important until the 1970s.)

It is important not to under-estimate the concerted attack on the profit motive in the Swedish housing industry, as it was carried out in the mid-twentieth century. From an ideological perspective, the elimination of the profit motive is an egalitarian dream. Profits are considered bad for two reasons:

a) They add to the income of people who own businesses, while those who do not own businesses are left behind.
b) They represent a "surplus value" of the kind that Marxists will happily discuss (in theory) at great length.

In a nutshell, profits are the manifestation of capitalism in people's pocketbooks. Since free-market capitalism is to egalitarianism what water is to fire, the obvious egalitarian conclusion is that free-market capitalism must go.

Early on, in their pursuit of an absolutely egalitarian welfare state, the Myrdals got what they wanted from the Social Democrat government. In 1939 the government-issued, taxpayer-guaranteed home-construction loans financed 5 percent of all new apartment homes. In 1942 they paid for 100 percent of them.

The socialization of home construction is a great case in point of how the egalitarian pursuit of a designer society turns out in practice. In order to create an all-egalitarian society, the Myrdals needed full employment of all economic resources – hence constantly high GDP growth. In order to accomplish that, they needed to micro-manage how many children people had, as well as the conditions under which those children were raised (or else they would end up with too many "highly unfit" individuals that would only be a burden to society).

Having government plan every aspect of the average family's life would, in their mind, lead to a maximization of the genetic and social health of the workforce. In this context it was perfectly reasonable that government micro-managed the architecture of people's homes and the subdivisions where they were built. A high-standard physical environment would, according to the Myrdals, lead to a healthier childhood – and eventually a stronger workforce. A stronger workforce, in turn, would lead to higher growth, and more tax money to pay for the welfare state.

In other words, the argument is circular: egalitarianism needs growth; growth needs egalitarianism.

So long as the theory behind the egalitarian project is correct, this circular reasoning will produce perennial prosperity for everybody. The only problem is: the theory behind the egalitarian project is not correct. Government cannot replace the free market as the means of distribution. Government is no better than individual entrepreneurs at forecasting the future; on the contrary, its forecasting performance is often worse. As a result, government ends up missing the mark both in terms of time for completion and in terms of the budget. (How many government projects can you name that have come in under budget, ahead of schedule? How many entitlement programs remain within the original cost estimate that Congress discussed when the program was created?)

The Swedish Social Democrats forged ahead. They were clearly not satisfied with a nationalized school system, a single-payer health-care system, and a housing industry where the profit motive had been reduced to eccentricity. They put a lot of effort into getting government involved in, and gradually taking over, child care. In 1938 a government-commissioned report proposed vast expansion of child-care institutions and the addition of explicit pedagogical goals. They also suggested standardized, mandatory training for staff and full day care from the age of two. In 1944 the Swedish parliament passed a bill creating national child-care subsidies directly modeled after a proposal by Alva Myrdal.

In order to receive the subsidies, starting in 1945 kindergartens had to have teachers whose education complied with national standards. To further tighten control over kindergartens, in 1962 the Swedish parliament passed a law nationalizing all pre-school teacher colleges.

Other reforms aiming in the same welfare-statist direction:

- Tax-financed children's dental care (1938);
- Per-child cash benefits to mothers (1948);
- Nationalized, mandatory school curriculum (1955);
- Tax-funded, paid sick leave as the beginning of a fully-paid family-leave program (1955);
- Universal retirement security (1960).[17]

With socialized health and child care and with other cash and in-kind reforms in rapid expansion, by the late 1950s the welfare statists were confident they had found the superior alternative to free-market capitalism.

Notes

1 Galbraith (2012).
2 One could make the case that the Soviet Union was a gigantic experiment in absolute egalitarianism. However, since Europe's Social Democrats were, at the same time, passionate supporters of egalitarianism and among the strongest opponents to communism during the twentieth century, it would be unfair to suggest that their pursuit of egalitarianism had much in common with the totalitarian systems east of the Iron Curtain.
3 Erixon (2008) and Erixon (2010).
4 As an anecdote showing the meticulous attention to detail in central planning: walking through some of the subdivision built in the 1960s and 1970s, one can easily spot "avenues" between the houses where building cranes ran back and forth on temporary rails to deliver construction material at breakneck speed.
5 Heckscher (1984).
6 For those proficient in Swedish, see especially Chapter 6 of the original Swedish version.
7 The author's translation.
8 Hirdman (1994).
9 Kap (2008, 2009).
10 The numerical reference 1950:70 represents a Swedish law, passed by parliament in 1950. It would have been the 70th law of that legislative session, hence the numerical reference.

11 Harris (1920).
12 Stewart (1934).
13 Cox (1921).
14 It is important to note, though, that the American health-reform debate is characterized by a large degree of ignorance on behalf of health socialization advocates. With the transition from market-based health care to a single-payer system, the conditions of health-care delivery fundamentally change. Access to health care is institutionally restricted in a way that Americans in general are not used to, and probably cannot fully comprehend without a detailed examination of real-world cases of destructive health-care rationing.
15 See www.allmannyttan.se/historia/historiska-epoker/1931-1945-allmannyttans-bostadspolitiska-roll-formas/ (accessed May 18, 2017).
16 See primarily sections on housing policies in Chapters 5 and 6.
17 In his 1958 book *Beyond the Welfare State*, Myrdal refers to the new government-run retirement security system as "a final effort to complete the edifice of social security ... aimed at eradicating what are almost the last remnants of" a so-called class society (p. 48).

4

EXPORTING EGALITARIANISM TO AMERICA

Looking at Sweden from the perspective of the Johnson administration, it is understandable that they thought its egalitarian project was a success. Some 25 years into its life, the Swedish welfare state was institutionally complete, and the nation's economy was outgrowing the U.S. economy. In fact, by the time President Johnson's War on Poverty working group pieced together his package of entitlement programs, Sweden was in the middle of a historic growth spurt that lasted for several more years. On average, the Swedish GDP grew by 4.7 percent annually throughout the 1960s.

By comparison, the U.S. economy, which was not taxed at nearly the same rates as the Swedish economy, "only" grew by 4.3 percent per year during the same period.

Unless one takes the RM economic-policy model into context, it is difficult to understand how a higher-taxed economy with a bigger government can outgrow an economy that is much more free-market oriented. However, the combination of, on the one hand, RM-model-based policies for "solidarity in wages" and promotion of exports and, on the other hand, a very ambitious, centrally planned home-construction program allowed the Swedish welfare state to surpass the U.S. economy for a sustained period of time.

By the turn of the 1970s Sweden ranked among the four wealthiest nations in the world.

From an ideological viewpoint, the early macroeconomic and institutional success of the welfare state should have been enough to allow the welfare statists to rest on their laurels, at least for a while. However, it is important to remember that the ideological prime directive of the Swedish welfare state, as declared in *The Demographic Crisis*, is not just egalitarianism, but *absolute* egalitarianism. This means, plain and simple, that the expansion of economic redistribution programs will not stop until all citizens are – literally – equal in economic outcomes.

Few people were aware of the relentlessness in government expansion as Gunnar Myrdal. His 1958 Storr Lectures at Yale University, published in his book *Beyond the Welfare State*, conveyed a strong sense of confidence in that government could, and would, continue to grow. At the same time, despite the undeniable success of the Rehn-Meidner economic model in supporting the welfare state, Myrdal somehow realized that even those policies would have their limitations. He predicted that the welfare state would eventually run out of sufficient tax revenue under the hybrid system of a limited free-market sector and indicative, central economic planning.

As a remedy for these limitations, Myrdal foresaw an end to the free-market part of the Swedish economy. He was, in fact, so confident in the virtues of unending government expansion that he predicted that Sweden would eventually part with free-market capitalism altogether. Instead, the country would adopt a hardline, Soviet-style central planning.[1]

Myrdal saw Soviet-style economic planning as the logical extension – or elevation – of the "measures" taken by the Swedish government to build and operate the welfare state. In *Beyond the Welfare State*, he explains how obvious he thought the path toward central economic planning really should be to everyone (p. 14):

> The development towards economic planning, in all the Western countries, has had its course demarcated by such intermittent attempts to bring more order and rationality to those measures of state intervention which had already grown up in a particular field. For a long time, these attempts at coordination were often – as they often still are – limited in scope. As a rule, they did not go far towards a permanent solution. New acts of state intervention, again usually assumed to be of only a temporary nature, were continually added, and soon diminished even the attained modicum of coordination.

Myrdal is far too humble. Intentionally or not, he downplays the coordinated effort behind the construction of the Swedish welfare state. That, however, does not diminish Myrdal's case for central economic planning: its motivation is not in the pursuit of central planning as an end goal, but as an instrument toward absolute egalitarianism. In other words, absolute egalitarianism requires central economic planning. The welfare state is just a stepping stone.

Once central planning became a reality, Myrdal suggested, the economic path to absolute egalitarianism would be straight, fast and irreversible.

It is worth noting, right here, that Myrdal's prediction turned out to be wrong. Sweden stopped just short of introducing Soviet-style economic planning. So did every other welfare state outside of what used to be the Soviet sphere in Eastern Europe. The egalitarian project slowed down markedly in the 1970s and 1980s.

The immediate reason why central planning never became a reality in the West is that it fell into well-deserved disrepute when practiced in the Soviet sphere. The

Soviet Union and its European satellites simply could not compete with the free-market based economies in Western Europe. As a result, not even the most fervent egalitarians in the West had much to gain from proposing Soviet-style central planning.

Even the Swedish welfare state ran into a roadblock, but not until after the failure of a sophisticated effort to create central planning through the political back door. After the final touches were added to the Swedish welfare state's entitlement roster in the 1960s, the Social Democrats began preparing for the next phase, including central economic planning. They spent most of the 1970s developing, marketing and trying to gain approval of a major plan to take over privately owned businesses. A system of tax-paid funds would gradually buy up shares in the biggest corporations, effectively and gradually turning them into government property.

The socialization plans met massive protests from the business community, so massive that the Social Democrats eventually scaled back their plans. After a six-year hiatus in opposition from 1976, their 1982 election victory allowed them to introduce a watered-down version of their socialization funds.

A decade later the center-right coalition that won the 1991 election dismantled those funds, ostensibly shutting the door forever on Soviet-style central planning in Sweden.

That, however, does not mean that egalitarians have stopped pursuing a bigger role for government. The expansion has slowed down, and in some cases been brought to a halt altogether, thanks to widespread austerity in Europe. Since the late 1970s, many European countries have used austerity programs to try to close persistent budget gaps. While their efforts have been futile in terms of the deficit, they have, at least temporarily, brought welfare-state expansion to a halt.[2]

Welfare-state expansion is also dependent on the original purpose for which the welfare state was created. Not all welfare states share the same ideological foundation:

- *The Demographic Crisis* defined the foundation of the Swedish welfare state and set it out on a course to absolute egalitarianism – a path that eventually would require the abandonment of free-market capitalism.
- The founding document of the British welfare state, known as the *Beveridge Report*, aimed to preserve free-market capitalism but give it a compassionate amendment.

In fact, the Beveridge Report, authored as it was by a conservative politician, was inherently opposed to "too much" government.[3] The idea was to have government provide a passive safety net for those in poverty – in other words, to alleviate the hardship of poverty. Unlike the Myrdals, Lord Beveridge distanced himself from such explicit egalitarian ideas as permanent income redistribution; government help was to be available only on passive terms. It was not the intention to make all citizens equal in outcomes. People who could provide for themselves would be expected to do so.

As if to emphasize the principled difference vs. the egalitarian welfare state, the Beveridge Report proposed leveling the playing field in terms of individual opportunity: all children should be provided a common educational foundation.

By focusing on equality in opportunity rather than equality in outcome, the British welfare state steered clear of permanent economic redistribution. That, in turn, is the very goal of egalitarianism and has been the true reason for the Swedish welfare state's existence.

If we could ask the founders of the British and the Swedish welfare state a simple question, "When is government big enough?" the answers would be illuminatingly different:

- Gunnar Myrdal would firmly state "when all economic differences between citizens are eliminated."
- Lord Beveridge, the author of the Beveridge Report, would reply "when poverty no longer means abject suffering."

The difference between these two questions, and their answers, is also the difference between the American welfare state before and after President Johnson's War on Poverty declaration. From his 1964 State of the Union speech onward, the American welfare state was founded on an egalitarian ambition with much in common with the Swedish welfare state. Like its Swedish equivalent, the American welfare state is an open-ended commitment to government expansion.

This comparison raises an obvious question: if they are so alike ideologically, why did the Swedish welfare state expand almost to completion in 20 years, while the American welfare state still has not added single-payer health care, universal child care and general income security to its entitlement roster?

One answer to that question has to do with the different systems of government in the two countries. According to Gunnar Myrdal, the Swedish welfare state maintained its momentum because of parliamentary democracy. Unlike the American federal constitutional republic, the parliamentary system is national, unicameral and built with, at most, two branches of government. (The Swedish constitution does not even provide an independent judiciary, placing all legislative, executive and de facto judicial power in the hands of parliament.) Furthermore, the parliamentary system lacks the minority-opinion safeguards that are built into the American system; there is practically unlimited trust in the ability of the majority to exercise unlimited powers with judicious limitations.

In reality, the Swedish parliamentary system allowed for a highly expedited roll-out of the egalitarian project. The roll-out was also facilitated by the combination of unicameral, centralized powers and a rapid increase in consumption of entitlements among the general population. Myrdal noted that once the idea that government can redistribute income and consumption has set root among the general public, voters will be more interested in those functions of government than the protection of life, liberty and property. Therefore, Myrdal explains (1958, p. 27):

> The urge for economic equalisation is everywhere present, and it is commonly proclaimed as a principle. Its sphere of operation is not limited to taxation and to redistributional expenditure schemes like those for various forms of social insurance. It enters into, and determines, the scope of all other state intervention. The important thing is that it then becomes one of the main driving forces behind the general trend towards increasing the volume of state intervention.

He then explains that there is no upper limit to the growth of the welfare state, simply because when the "less privileged groups" realize that they can use the means of parliamentarianism to further their own interests, they will press for subordinating the free market and the pursuit of individual interests to "laws, regulations, administrative dispositions" and other instruments by which government seizes more control over the economy and people's lives.

In plain words, the pursuit of absolute egalitarianism is not ideological radicalism – it is the logical consequence of democracy. When private relations become public, says Myrdal, low-income voters are more confident that their interests will be put highest on the political agenda. Eventually, he states confidently, this combination of egalitarian economic redistribution and universal suffrage will bring all political opponents of the welfare state to their knees:

> Even the conservative and liberal parties will have to become the vehicles for this development, or else disappear from the political scene.

In other words, parliamentary democracy helps straighten the route to absolute egalitarianism. Under a system of government where the majority vote is closely safeguarded but the opinions of the minority are ignored, the pursuit of egalitarianism becomes a self-propelling phenomenon. The welfare state, gradually expanding its entitlement programs, over time provides benefits for a growing segment of the population. As more and more people see the opportunity to benefit from the welfare state, they line up behind welfare-statist alternatives in elections. Perpetuating governments with a redistributive agenda, voters thereby fuse the pursuit of egalitarianism with parliamentary democracy.

Traditional European parliamentarianism is particularly vulnerable to an egalitarian takeover. Its majority-rules principle lacks the checks and balances that are built into the American constitutional republic. By separating powers, the U.S. Constitution puts brakes on ideological runaway movements. It also inhibits the kind of fusion between the system of government and one particular ideology by enumerating the powers of the federal government vs. the states and the people. Generally speaking, no such enumeration exists in European parliamentary democracies.

By providing for the protection of minority opinions, the U.S. Constitution also recognizes that individuals are equal in opportunity but not in values and ideas. This recognition does not exist in the practice of European parliamentary democracy. The strict European majority-rules principle presumes that all individuals are equal to a much larger extent than the American system of government. That presumption includes the sharing of basic values, or the acceptance of the values of the majority once the parliamentary process has concluded with a majority vote. All individuals are then implicitly expected to endorse the opinion of the majority and live happily ever after. The individual is subordinate to the collective.

Does this mean that the American system of government will eventually prove to be an overwhelming adversary for the egalitarian project?

The answer to this question is "no." It is undeniably the case that parliamentary democracy provides strong institutional support for the welfare state. According to Myrdal, the combination of egalitarianism and parliamentarianism is strong enough to overpower any resistance that comes naturally with the free market. However, the path to absolute egalitarianism does not have to be revolutionary; a piecemeal approach is likely to be at least as successful, allowing the egalitarian project to fly under the conservative political radar.

Myrdal actually suggests that the piecemeal approach can achieve the same total transformation of a society as the Soviet revolution did. The idea of central economic planning, he says, springs from the piecemeal growth of government in education, health care and income security. This gradual expansion of the welfare state "again and again" proves its opponents wrong; it is not possible, Myrdal suggests, to identify any adverse economic effects of expanding government. Therefore, the expansion can safely continue. At some point, though, their sheer volume and complexity will call for a higher level of administration. All entitlement programs, all taxes and all associated regulatory measures simply reach a critical mass where government can no longer run them by conventional means. Inevitably, Myrdal explains, a welfare state reaches the point where central economic planning must replace the free-market base in the economy (1958, p. 47).

Egalitarianism in America

After a very expansive start in the 1960s, the egalitarian American welfare state slowed its expansion markedly. It stopped short of creating programs such as universal child care; paid family leave, which was beginning to make it through state legislatures a half century after the War on Poverty started; and single-payer health care, also known as the crown jewel of the welfare state. To some degree, Congress has replaced actual entitlement programs with regulations, forcing private citizens to spend their money according to political preferences. The mandate under the Affordable Care Act forcing all Americans to buy health insurance could be described as a "diet" version of single-payer health care.

Overall, though, the institutional expansion of the American welfare state slowed to a crawl once Congress had created and modified the entitlement programs introduced and expanded under the War on Poverty. Only three major entitlement programs have been created since then: the Earned Income Tax Credit, which was part of President Ford's Tax Reduction Act; the State Child Health Insurance Program, created under President Clinton; and President Obama's Affordable Care Act.

Attempts at rolling back the welfare state are almost non-existent. In 1996 President Clinton signed the Personal Responsibility and Work Opportunity Reconciliation Act – also known as PRWORA or Welfare Reform – the purpose of which was to rein in cost increases in welfare programs. That is about as close as America has come to reversing the egalitarian project. Overall, the welfare state has remained institutionally stable and continued to fulfill its purpose of economic redistribution.

One piece of evidence showing the steady growth in the welfare state is the increase in the dependency of American families on tax-paid transfers:

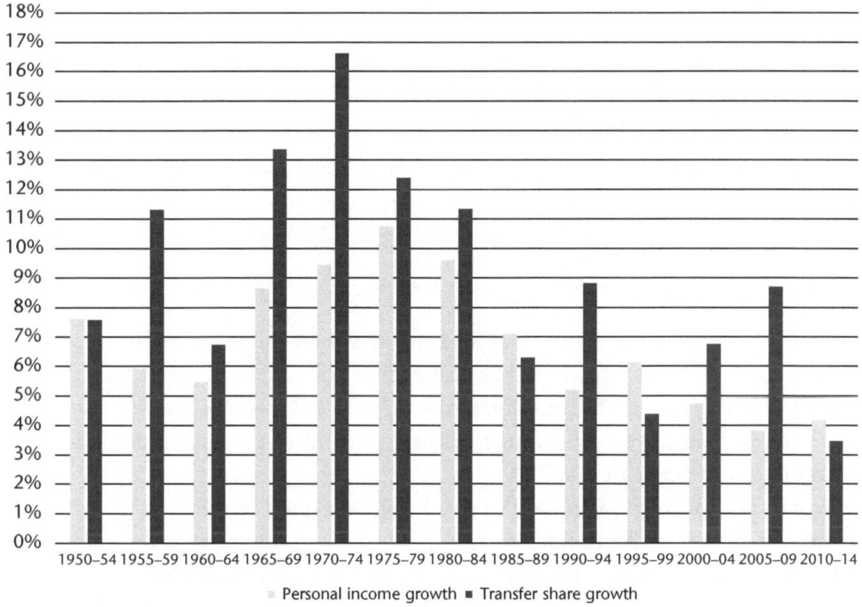

FIGURE 4.1 Growth: personal current transfers and personal income: current prices, 5-year average

Source: Bureau of Economic Analysis

Or, viewed differently:

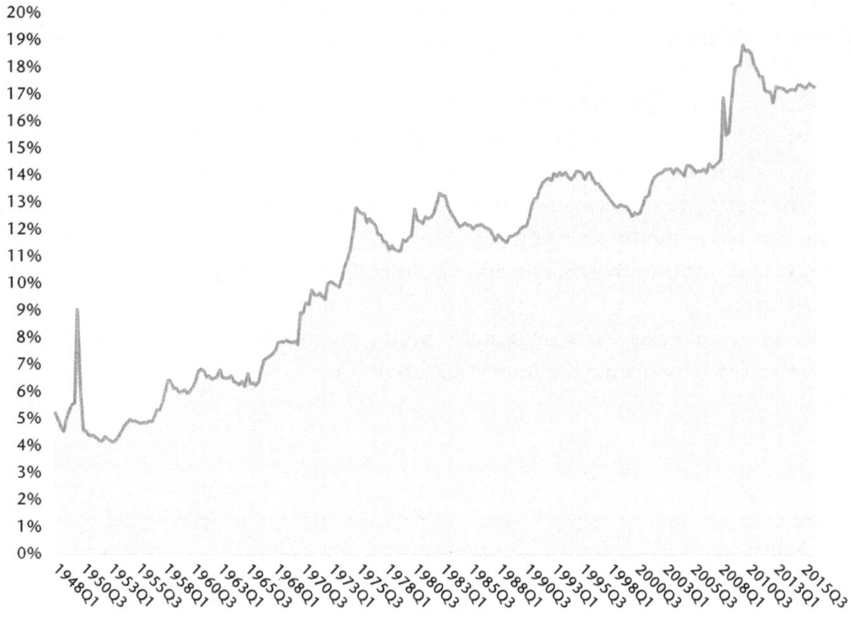

FIGURE 4.2 Personal current transfers as share of personal income: United States

Source: Bureau of Economic Analysis

Before the War on Poverty, Social Security was responsible for the lion's share of transfers to households. However, because of the limited demographic that receives Social Security checks, the transfer share of personal income grew very slowly before the War on Poverty: from just below 5 percent of personal income in 1955 to a bit over 6 percent in 1965.

By contrast, once the War on Poverty began, tax-paid transfers rapidly became an influential part of household finances. By 1975 transfers were responsible for 12.5 percent of all personal income. Since then, the share has continued to increase and is currently (late 2016) floating just above 17 percent.

As evidence of how successful President Johnson's egalitarian project has been, as of 2016 more than two thirds of all personal transfer payments from government to American households come from other entitlement programs than Social Security.

In short: income redistribution is working, and it is having a significant effect on how U.S. families pay for their regular expenses. This would probably not have happened, had the American welfare state been built on the British socially conservative Beveridge Report, rather than the same foundations as the Swedish welfare state is built on.

There is a direct lineage from the ideological cornerstones of the War on Poverty back to the Myrdals. The link is in the works of American economist John Kenneth Galbraith. A legend among the academic left, Galbraith wrote several books about political economy, economic policy and related issues. His career strongly resembles that of Gunnar Myrdal, with a scholarly and political interest transcending economic, political and social issues. Like Myrdal, Galbraith was also active in both academia and public policy. For example:

- Myrdal held an endowed chair in political economy at the Stockholm School of Economics and co-founded the Institute for International Economic Studies at the University of Stockholm; he was a member of parliament and served in Prime Minister Erlander's cabinet; after World War II he served as executive secretary of the United Nations Commission on Europe.
- Galbraith was a faculty member at Harvard for half a century; he was the United States ambassador to India under President Kennedy and served in the administrations of four U.S. presidents, among them Lyndon Johnson.

His ideological views were also close to Myrdal's, though not quite as radical.

Galbraith and Myrdal were friends, to the extent to which Myrdal sent Galbraith his travel itineraries when visiting the United States.[4] There is no doubt that this contributed to the influence that Myrdal had on Galbraith's work; even though the exact level of influence is hard to pinpoint, one can recognize some of Myrdal's thoughts in Galbraith's writings. In *The New Industrial State*, first published in 1967, Galbraith discusses the role of economic planning in the U.S. economy in terms not dissimilar from those that Myrdal uses in *Beyond the Welfare State* (1958). Galbraith does not go as far as to share Myrdal's affinity for teleological, central planning, but there is little doubt that his advocacy of an elaborate form of indicative economic planning, roughly comparable to the RM model, was inspired by Myrdal.

Galbraith's relationship with President Lyndon Johnson was very close, at a level where the President on at least one occasion summoned him to the White House for help with speech writing. Galbraith's book *The Affluent Society*, published in 1958, has been credited as a major source of inspiration for President Johnson's anti-poverty policies.[5] Galbraith was also part of the team that actually designed the War on Poverty, primarily through the 1964 Economic Opportunity Act.[6] In effect, Galbraith was a leading contributor to the ideological redefinition of the U.S. welfare state.

A key element in the redefinition effort was the adoption of the change in the definition of poverty from absolute to relative. The originator of this concept was Social Security Administration economist Mollie Orshansky, whose contributions allowed the War on Poverty working group to give their entitlement programs a clearly egalitarian orientation. Orshansky's relative poverty concept removed limitations on entitlement spending that had previously confined them to relief of poverty. Once President Johnson signed the Economic Opportunity Act, with which his War on Poverty went from theory to practice, America's entitlement programs began comprehensively and permanently redistribute income and consumption.

With all the similarities between the U.S. and Swedish welfare states, it is important to once again note the differences. The fact that the United States still does not have a single-payer health-care system, or a universal paid-family-leave program, could be interpreted as a sign that American egalitarianism has lost steam. While not being rolled back, has it reached its maximum potential?

Part of the answer to this question lies, again, in the constitutional differences between the United States and Europe in general (and Sweden in particular). Gunnar Myrdal was clear on this point: he saw the European unitary-state parliamentary model as a form of government more favorable to the egalitarian project. That model has a strong central government and puts complete faith in the majority-rules principle; anywhere it is practiced, the welfare state has grown faster and larger than it has in the United States.

According to Myrdal, the reason for the successful combination of parliamentarianism and the welfare state is rather simple. When the welfare state grows, people become more dependent on it for more and more functions in their lives. As they do, they are more inclined to vote to perpetuate as well as to expand the welfare state.

There is no doubt that this is a valid explanation of why egalitarians were so successful in rapidly building the welfare state, especially in the smaller countries in Scandinavia. However, as the welfare state grows, people other than its immediate beneficiaries have to pay higher taxes. Unless they are overwhelmed ideologically, as Heckscher (1984) explains, it is perfectly reasonable to expect them to vote against further expansion of the welfare state.

Here, the majority-rules principle goes to work. The legislative procedure gives right of way to a majority ruling, with few or no safeguards to let minority opinions stall or inhibit the passing of legislative bills. Typically, the passage of a bill requires one vote in a unicameral parliament. Furthermore, the executive power is appointed by the legislative body, and therefore automatically reflects the same values and opinions as the parliamentary majority.

Lastly, the judicial branch typically lacks authority to try cases against entitlement programs. The cases brought in U.S. courts against the Affordable Care Act would be unthinkable in unicameral, unitary-state systems that most European countries are so fond of.

The said litigation did not reverse the Affordable Care Act, but the Supreme Court ruling in 2012 in favor of the insurance-purchase mandate of the Act (*NFIB v. Sebelius*), together with other litigation efforts likely discouraged both President Obama and welfare-statist members of Congress from pursuing other major entitlement programs. It also led to the Republicans winning a Senate majority in 2014 – thereby completely controlling the legislative branch – and to Donald Trump's victory in the 2016 presidential election.

The shifts in Republican favor in 2014 and 2016 were to some degree similar to them taking control over Congress after President Clinton's failed attempt at creating a single-payer health-care system with his 1993 Health Security Act. However, when Clinton came back in 1997 with SCHIP (State Children's Health Insurance Program) there was no visible reaction at all among the electorate. In other words, while Clinton wanted the American welfare state to take a major leap forward, he eventually settled with a small step. But the motion was still forward, not backward.

By separating powers and by having an open-litigation system, the U.S. Constitution has clearly slowed down the progress of egalitarianism in America. The welfare state still plays a smaller role in the American economy than it does in Europe:

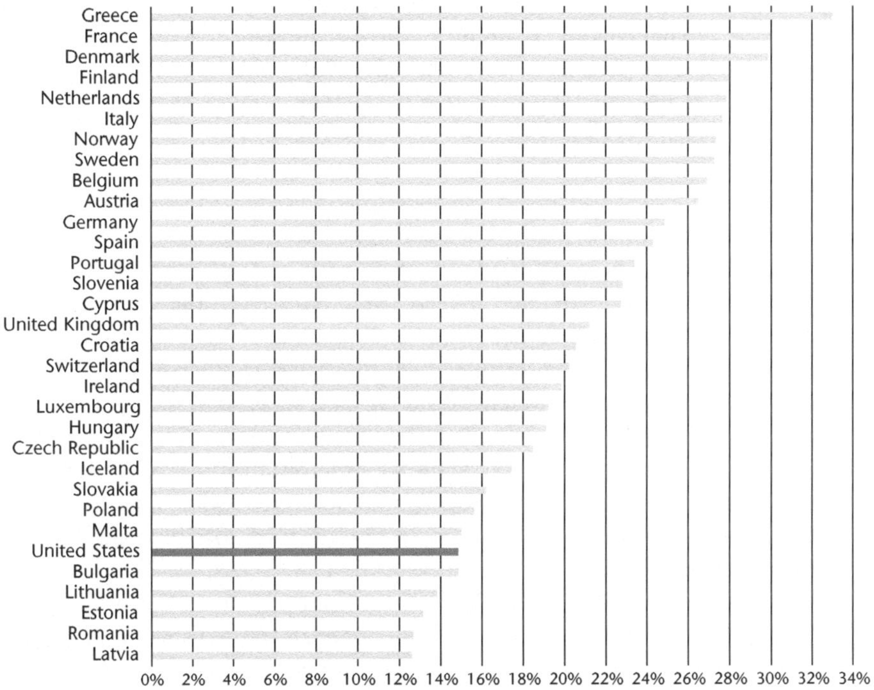

FIGURE 4.3 Social protection expenditures, share of GDP, 2015

Source: Eurostat (European countries): Office of Management and Budget and Bureau of Economic Analysis (United States)

It is important to note that the comparatively slow progress of the American welfare state is not a sign that Americans want their welfare state reversed. Republicans, who could be expected to be somewhat skeptical of the welfare state, prefer candidates in primaries and general elections who have nothing against growing government control, so long as it happens slowly. Their support for a welfare-state gradualism of sorts is exemplified by President Reagan's numerous approvals of entitlement expansions, and by George W Bush's signature Medicare expansion.

While it is too early to definitively speak to President Trump's ambitions on the welfare-state front, it is reasonable to expect that he will continue the tread-slowly tradition. A good guess would be that he at some point signs a bill expanding the federal government's role in child care, and that he will allow the creation of a federal paid-family-leave program.

Three fundamental problems with the American welfare state

Since American conservatives are apparently unwilling or unable to produce a comprehensive alternative to egalitarianism, and since Republicans in office tend to approve of an enumerated expansion of the welfare state, it is crucial that they – together with their friends on the left side of the aisle – acknowledge and consider the three structural problems that the welfare state is suffering from. The following three chapters deal with these problems, one by one:

1 Fiscal Eugenics: the welfare state reduces the individual to an instrument for collectivist government policies; as a consequence, the sacrosanctity of life, and the inviolability of personal freedom and property are replaced with an instrumentalist definition of life, liberty and property; the unintentional consequence of this subordination of the individual is that government, with good intentions, removes principled firewalls against totalitarianism.
2 Slow Growth: under the weight of the welfare state, all Western economies have gradually drifted into, or in proximity to, a state of macroeconomic stagnation; children grow up to a life less prosperous than that of their parents; economic progress is replaced with economic regress, with potentially very serious consequences for the future economic and social stability of the American society.
3 Endless Debt: caused partly by slow growth, partly by the inherent design of the welfare state, Western countries are suffering from increasingly urgent government debt problems; budget deficits have de facto become a permanent funding source for the welfare state; the consequences are short term – fiscal panic – and long term, where our debt burden robs our children of the prosperity they could otherwise have enjoyed.

Notes

1 The Soviet version of central economic planning is often referred to simply as "central planning." Technically, it is known as teleological planning; the difference between this type of planning and indicative planning is that the latter relies on free-market mechanisms for pricing and allocation of everyday goods and services. By contrast, teleological planning uses a centrally administered pricing system for all goods and services.

2 Larson (2014), Chapters 4a and 4b.
3 Beveridge (1942).
4 See the John Kenneth Galbraith collection at the John F Kennedy Library in Boston, Mass.
5 Gallaway and Garrett (2016).
6 Abramsky (2014).

5

PROBLEM 1

Fiscal Eugenics

In order to reduce, minimize and eventually eradicate socio-economic differences between individuals, the egalitarian must create government systems that reconfigure the economy in terms of how income and wealth are distributed among the citizenry. For this purpose, a welfare state is created with entitlements, and progressive taxation to pay for them. The welfare state is a system of economic redistribution built according to the egalitarian ideological blueprint. Part of this blueprint defines the relationship between the individual and the collective, represented by the state.

In a libertarian society, the individual is sovereign with an absolute right to his life and his property. His rights rise above the powers of the state, which makes life sacrosanct and property inviolable. For clarity, a person's right to property includes the proceeds of his work, and since the right is absolute, it cannot be abridged; in short, he has an inviolable right to the full proceeds of his work.[1]

By contrast, in an egalitarian society the individual's rights are subordinated to the powers of the state. This makes them conditional, with the conditions defining the extent of his rights being decided by the state. If the state finds use for a person's property that, according to the state, has a higher value, then by the egalitarian moral playbook the state is right in seizing whatever share of the person's property it deems appropriate.

From an analytical viewpoint, it is not controversial that egalitarianism allows the state to confiscate – namely, tax – people's property. There is, of course, always room for argument whether or not the economic consequences of egalitarianism are good or bad, but there is no room for controversy over the fact that egalitarianism prescribes taxation for the purposes of economic redistribution. In other words, the contrast between the rights hierarchy under, respectively, libertarianism and egalitarianism is clear. Concentrating, again, on the right to property:

- Libertarianism ranks the individual above the state; the individual's right supersedes any needs of the state; the individual's right is inviolable.
- Egalitarianism ranks the state above the individual; the individual's right is subordinated to the needs of the state; the individual's right is conditional.

To libertarians, the same rights hierarchy applies to the right to life. One would expect that egalitarianism would show the same respect for life, elevating it to sacrosanct status. However, in its practice under the welfare state, egalitarianism actually applies the same hierarchy to life as it does to property. Put simply yet accurately, the extent of the individual's control over his own life is subordinate to the welfare state's over-arching egalitarian goals.

The origins of egalitarian eugenics

In their book *The Demographic Crisis*, Gunnar and Alva Myrdal make plentiful use of the egalitarian moral hierarchy. People are referred to as "the population stock" and "demographic material" that the state has the right – even the obligation – to reconfigure. As abstract as this may sound, it is a public-policy practice that, back in the twentieth century, became known as eugenics. The idea of weeding out weak individuals from the population stock was not original to the Myrdals, but essential to the socialist Fabian Society of early-twentieth-century Britain. To them, eugenics was a perfectly acceptable, even necessary practice. According to Dennis Sewell (2009), writing for *The Spectator*, the Fabians wanted to prevent the poor from, so to speak, outbreeding the middle class, as this would cause "degeneration of the gene pool." Eugenics was a policy tool, essential to their political ideology, by means of which they believed they could exercise nationwide demographic planning.

In fact, says Sewell, the Fabians wanted government to create a gene-pool task force of sorts, charged with "weeding out" individuals deemed to be "unfit":[2]

> Those who were found wanting by these tribunals were to be segregated in special colonies or sterilised. One politician who supported such draconian measures in parliament was the Labour MP Will Crooks, who described the targets of the eugenics campaign as 'like human vermin' who 'crawl about doing absolutely nothing, except polluting and corrupting everything they touch'.

Sewell also reports of speculation at one Eugenics Society meeting of how government could "use a 'lethal chamber' to solve the problem" of genetically unwanted individuals. Given the history of the twentieth century, it is not difficult to see what this line of thinking could have accomplished, had it won more support in wider political circles in Britain. As it turned out, it was another European government that put the idea of "lethal chambers" to work for eugenic purposes.

That said, one should not under-estimate the influence of the socialist Fabian Society on early-twentieth-century British politics. The founders of the Fabian Society authored one of the most important British government reports of the early twentieth century, namely the Minority Report of the Royal Commission on the Poor Laws. Published in 1909, this report has been acclaimed as one of two pillars of twentieth-century British welfare policy, the other being the Beveridge Report of 1942.

As explained earlier, Gunnar and Alva Myrdal applied a thick layer of eugenics thinking to the development of the Swedish welfare state. Their argument for "weeding out" weak character traits from the "population stock" was that in doing so, government would maximize the productivity of the Swedish workforce. Thereby, sustained levels of high growth would produce a maximum of tax revenue for the welfare state to spend.

Most of the eugenic elements of *The Demographic Crisis* were focused on getting government involved in people's lives, to a point where government de facto took over the responsibility for raising children. Parents were to be retained for breed-and-feed services.

That is, if they were allowed to breed. The Swedish eugenic practice of sterilization has been documented by Alberto Spektorowski of the Gordon Faculty of Social Sciences at Tel Aviv University, and Elisabet Mizrachi, then a graduate student at Tel Aviv University.[3] In an important article from 2004, Spektorowski and Mizrachi carefully document the use of sterilization for eugenic purposes under the Swedish welfare state. Over a 40-year period, from 1935 to 1975, more than 62,000 individuals were sterilized, a frightening number for any welfare state. Not surprisingly, Spektorowski and Mizrachi explain, this practice has earned Sweden notoriety (p. 333):

> The extent to which sterilization was performed on physically healthy individuals … was far greater than in all other Nordic countries with similar law. It was the only country with a state eugenic society, and among the Nordic countries it was the one where eugenics met with its greatest success.

Convincingly, they also link the practice of sterilization in Sweden to the eugenics developed by the British socialist Fabian Society (p. 334):

> [A]lthough the ideological core of the Swedish social democracy remained reformist and stressed the humanist or idealist elements of Marxist thought, there were strong tendencies towards a Fabian concept of industrial democracy and an exclusionist concept of social welfare, serving as a basis for social eugenics. Deprived of mythical and romantic racist features, the basic idea of eugenic socialism was to engineer a welfare community for 'the fittest' or a 'welfare eugenics', built on parameters of 'right-living' destined to exclude those individuals defined as non-productive.

This is a good summary of the productivity thinking behind the prophylactic social policy that the Myrdals made such a big point of in *The Demographic Crisis*, and that was also a guideline for the RM-economic policy model. Spektorowski and Mizrachi note that the welfare-state form of eugenics emphasized "efficiency, productivism and social margins" as opposed to genetic characteristics. Under the scientific socialism that defines the welfare state's political practice,

> the determining factor for exclusion from the community was not race but the productive capacity of a member of society. Non-productive elements were denied not social welfare, but their right to procreate.

Individuals who possess characteristics that government deems undesirable – such as low productivity – are thus forced to subordinate their lives to the will of the state. Under the practice of eugenic sterilization, their lives did not end, but their bloodline did.

Regardless of whether sterilization was practiced for the reasons given by the socialist Fabian Society, or under the welfare state as specified by the Myrdals, the practice explicitly demoted the individual to a moral status below the state. An ideology, be it socialist Darwinism, racism as practiced in Nazi Germany, or the welfare state, puts conditions on the very life conditions of an individual.

One would expect that the practice of reducing individual lives to instruments for a government-imposed purpose had disappeared with World War II, or at least with the end of forced sterilization in Sweden (which again ended in 1975). However, the moral ranking model that egalitarians apply through the welfare state is still very much alive. In order to achieve egalitarian political goals, the welfare state is ready to dispense with select categories of individuals.

The selection mechanism is technically different, but its consequences are no less damning for those whose lives are deselected.

Fiscal eugenics

It is important not to use "eugenics" casually. As with other charged terms, prolific employment of it easily drains the term, and the actions that really qualify as eugenics, of their true meaning. The 40 years of government-sanctioned sterilization in Sweden was, in intent and effect, eugenics, and should be classified as such. Sparse use of the term then builds a barrier between morally reprehensible government policies and what can qualify as the morally tolerable, acceptable and approvable.

When the term "eugenics" is applied casually, it waters down the authoritarian nature of government policies that separate "desirable" human characteristics from "non-desirable" ones. To use the terminology provided by Spektorowski and Mizrachi: the distinction between eugenic and non-eugenic policies is the distinction between exclusionary and non-exclusionary policies. In a welfare state, the consequences of exclusion are government-imposed denials of fundamental experiences, at the level exemplified by the Swedish sterilization program.

There are striking examples of when the term "eugenics" is misused and thereby blurs the exclusionary demarcation line. For example, it has been suggested that welfare reform of 1996, also known by its acronym PRWORA, was motivated by eugenics.[4] Yet even a brief examination of PRWORA proves that it was not at all an example of eugenics. The 1996 welfare reform act aimed at incentivizing certain behavior, and discouraging other behavior, among some people whose daily livelihood depended on government money. In terms of personal characteristics, the group targeted by welfare reform was selected because of their dependency on welfare; no other characteristics applied in the identification of the group. In other words, no racial or other genetic variables were relevant in the design or execution of PRWORA.

Welfare reform aimed to discourage perpetual dependency on government. Its criteria for terminating welfare under its lifetime government-dependency cap were behavioral in nature. Such criteria as race, gender or disabilities are existential in nature; when the Swedish government sterilized people, it did so based on existential criteria, not people's behavior.

To be blunt, when government applies personal character traits as a sorting mechanism, the person is assumed *a priori* to behave in a certain way – and therefore tagged as "desirable" or "undesirable." Individuals with the "undesirable" character traits can behave however they want; government has already branded them.

Under PRWORA, individual actions, not character traits, determine their path through and beyond the program. The default assumption is that everyone can succeed in becoming economically independent.

Under eugenics, individual character traits, not actions, predispose individuals to a future as a productive, or non-productive, citizen. The default assumption is that character traits, not actions, determine success.

The most notorious example of the practice of eugenics in the twentieth century took place in the Third Reich. The Nazis created a template for the characteristics of an individual that would be deemed desirable or acceptable as a member of the German people. In order to make the people of Germany fit that template, the Nazis resorted to population re-engineering – or the sorting of individuals on character-based criteria. Under the eugenic policy principle of *lebensunwertes leben* ("life unworthy of living") the Nazis set out to clean the German population of individuals whose lives were considered a burden to society. The principle said that a person with genetic characteristics beyond a certain degree of severity would never be able to make a positive contribution to society, and should therefore be discarded.

Beyond their racist atrocities, the Nazis associated the unworthy-life policy with a cost-benefit analysis. An individual whose personal – primarily racial – characteristics predicted a productive life, were sorted into the "desirable" category; individuals whose characteristics predicted an unproductive life, were sorted out as "undesirable" and often targeted for euthanasia.

The link between, on the one hand, "desirable" and "undesirable" personal characteristics and, on the other hand, expected productivity was not something the Nazis invented. As mentioned, the socialist Fabian Society resorted to similar thinking, as did the Myrdals in 1934. But eugenic thinking was not confined to Europe: in 1937, Frederic Osborn, anthropologist and research associate at the American Museum of Natural History, published an article in the *American Sociological Review* about the then-current state of eugenics. Based on the materials presented at a eugenics conference held in New York that same year, Osborn suggests that physicians[5]

> should keep in close touch with the eugenist so that they will understand the eugenic implications of all medical work and its effect on the distribution of births. Doctors are in a position to influence a favorable distribution of births more perhaps than any other group.

In modern welfare states, eugenics is not race-based. Yet it is in health care that eugenic practices make themselves best known. The sorting mechanism for the provision and distribution of health care is no longer genetic, but fiscal. Scarce resources in government-run health-care systems force government to ration health care; the criteria for rationing become the sorting mechanism that replaces racial and other discrimination variables.

Rewritten to fit the fiscal version of eugenics, the quote from anthropologist Frederic Osborn would sounds something like this:

> [physicians] should keep in close touch with the economist so that they will understand the fiscal implications of all medical work and its effect on the distribution of scarce health-care resources. Doctors are in a position to influence a favorable distribution of scarce funds more perhaps than any other group.

To play on the German term for racist eugenics, this welfare-state version would be called *haushaltsunwertes leben*, a life unworthy of the government budget. The eugenicists that bring the egalitarian welfare state from theory to practice are preoccupied not with discarding genetically unfit individuals, but with separating individuals that fit the budget from individuals whose lives are deemed too costly.

Despite this difference in terms of end goal, fiscal eugenics shares the same disrespect for individual sovereignty that defines racist eugenics. It motivates the invasion of a person's daily life, such as but not limited to invading his bodily functions in the form of forced sterilization. The express purpose with the invasion is to make sure that every citizen, over his lifetime, has a net positive fiscal balance with government.

In other words, the welfare state raises two questions about the lives of individual citizens in relation to the government budget:

- If a person can be sterilized to prevent him or her from having children with the same genetic characteristics that government has deemed too costly, then how far is the step to forced abortions aimed at terminating the life of babies with unacceptably costly characteristics?

- If a person is exceptionally productive, with a capacity to produce significantly more than the average worker, should government minimize his free time and force him or her to work longer hours to maximize his output and thereby tax revenue?

These questions are not hypothetical. They are directly translatable to real-life situations. To begin with the first question, a full-fledged welfare state, which includes single-payer health care, builds a direct link between critically important health situations in people's lives and the government's budget. When government makes health-care promises to the entire population, by means of its single-payer system (without which no welfare state is complete), then those promises are in no way restricted or conditioned by government's ability to pay for those promises. Demand for health care will be based on the health needs of the population, while supply of health care is determined by the welfare state's tax base.

At this point, a welfare state is in jeopardy unless it can obtain a balance between health-care needs and tax revenue. This need for balance spans the entire portfolio of entitlements, from health care to education, child care, elderly care and income security; the discrepancy between entitlement demand and entitlement funding grows exponentially as the welfare state expands.

The Myrdals suggested their "prophylactic social policy" as a cure for this funding discrepancy. On the tax-revenue side, their policies sought to reconfigure the Swedish population into a more productive "human material." On the entitlement demand side, their ambition was to sort out and discard individuals and hereditary conditions that were "unfit" for the welfare state.

Few, if any, countries have been more doctrinaire than Sweden in complying with the welfare state "construction manual" provided in *The Demographic Crisis*. Consequently, Sweden went to greater length than other countries in reconfiguring its "human material"; the prolific sterilization program is one example. The problem, though, was that not even tight government control over education, income security, child care, home construction and other elements of a "prophylactic social policy" could sustain tax revenue where the welfare state needed it to be. As GDP growth slowed down during the 1970s, government began experiencing persistent fiscal problems. Since taxes had already been maximized, and the economy was dominated by major export industries (as per the RM-economic policy model), the only way to close the deficit gap was to ration the welfare state's entitlements.

At this point, the egalitarian project is faced with a pivotal question. The reason why people cannot get the health care promised to them is the egalitarian project – the welfare state – itself. Therefore, what matters more: the continuation of the egalitarian project, or the satisfaction of people's needs for health care?

The answer to this question is to be found in the egalitarian moral hierarchy, which subordinates the individual to the state, or the collective. To sharpen the moral problem:

- On the one hand, in its pursuit of egalitarianism, government has defaulted on some promises, leaving people – who had no choice but to trust those promises – with forcefully unsatisfied needs.
- On the other hand, the egalitarian ideology ranks the collective above the individual in terms of policy priorities, meaning that the individual's needs are less important than an egalitarian policy outcome.

So far, in welfare states that have gone through harsh episodes of austerity, the solution has been to defend and preserve the egalitarian system. Larson (2014) explains the difference between austerity that leads to a genuine reduction in government size, and statist austerity. The latter is a form of government spending cuts that are not coupled with tax cuts, but aimed squarely at downsizing the existing welfare state to fit inside a tighter tax base. In order to do so, government must ration entitlements; rationing in turn necessitates the default on at least some entitlement promises; since government maintains its structural monopoly on the services it provides as entitlements, those whose needs are left unfilled are sacrificed at the altar of egalitarianism. Morally, this means that the individual is subordinated to the welfare state. The preferences of the state supersede the needs of the individual.

Over time, as rationing of entitlements becomes an integrated part of welfare-state governance, government needs new methods to institutionalize rationing. This happens primarily in health care, where the discipline of medical ethics specializes in providing choice parameters for health-care rationing.

One of the most controversial examples is the argument for infanticide put forward by medical ethicists Alberto Giubilini and Francesca Minerva in a 2013 issue of the *Journal of Medical Ethics*.[6] The article bluntly suggests that mothers should be allowed to kill their newborn, disabled babies in order to relieve themselves – and society – of the burden and the cost of caring for them.

The article starts with a warm-up to the infanticide argument by shortening the moral distance between pre-birth abortion and post-birth abortion:

> Severe abnormalities of the fetus and risks for the physical and/or psychological health of the woman are often cited as valid reasons for abortion. Sometimes the two reasons are connected, such as when a woman claims that a disabled child would represent a risk to her mental health. However, having a child can itself be an unbearable burden for the psychological health of the woman or for her already existing children, regardless of the condition of the fetus. … A serious philosophical problem arises when the same conditions that would have justified abortion become known after birth. In such cases, we need to assess facts in order to decide whether the same arguments that

> apply to killing a human fetus can also be consistently applied to killing a newborn human. Such an issue arises, for example, when an abnormality has not been detected during pregnancy or occurs during delivery.

This argument fits squarely within the egalitarian ideology, and therefore becomes a policy guideline for the construction and operation of the welfare state.

At its core, egalitarianism is an elaborate form of utilitarian value theory. Every individual's needs are reduced to a utility function, the utility values of which are determined not by the individual himself, but by government.

If each individual determines his own utility function, and thereby values his own needs, then it is unlikely that two individuals will ever place the same value on the same need; one person may value a fun-driving car, while another prefers eating expensive and exotic-tasting meals. The first person will put more money into buying a car that meets his preferences; the second person will allocate a larger share of his budget to unusual, expensive culinary ingredients.

Likewise, one family prefers to spend a lot of money on preventative medicine, institutional child care and traditional school-based education for their children, while another family values traveling and homeschooling. The utility values that they attach to similar needs are very different.

In a welfare state, government will assume that those differences do not exist. It socializes education and provides a standardized classroom experience for every child, as if all families wanted the exact same education for their children. By the same token, government decides how much we all want to spend on preventative medicine and other products supplied by the welfare state. This standardization of our needs and their utility values is necessary for the successful execution of egalitarian policies: if government assumes that Jack and Jill want the exact same education for their children, then government can conveniently provide that education for them; there is no need to accommodate individual preferences.

The key to this standardization of needs and their values – utilities – is the separation of an individual's utility function from him as a person. Government must control the utility function, or else it cannot determine the utility that the individual citizen will experience from the entitlements that government provides.

The separation of a person's needs and their values from the person himself gives the person, or entity, in charge of the utility function full control over that person's life. Person B becomes the final arbiter of Person A's needs, down to such basics as food, shelter and clothing.

When health care is included in government's roster of entitlements, Person B ends up in charge of Person A's life-related needs.

This is where the pursuit of egalitarianism is morally related to the medical-ethics issue of legalized infanticide, also known as, post-birth abortion. The premise of the argument in favor of infanticide is that the mother has authority over the baby's utility function. She therefore has the right to decide that the baby's needs, current and future, have a lower total utility value than her own current and future needs. Therefore, the argument goes, she has the right to terminate the baby's life.

It could be objected that a newborn baby is unable to take responsibility for its own utility experiences, necessitating the transfer of authority over his utility function to someone else. However, this is an irrelevant point: if life is axiomatically inviolable, in other words, sacrosanct, then the mother's control over her baby's needs remains, but she is now confined to the responsibility of providing for those needs – not passing judgment on them.

Once Person A's utility function is placed under the jurisdiction of Person B, it is up to Person B to decide not only what needs Person A should have satisfied, but also what those needs cost and how to prioritize between them based on their cost. In their argument for infanticide, Giubilini and Minerva gradually approach this conclusion. As a step along the way they differentiate between children with Down's Syndrome and "normal" children; by placing a lower value on the needs of a child with Down's Syndrome, they argue not only for the abortion of those babies when diagnosed, but also for their infanticide. Based on data from 18 European health registries for the period 2005–2009, Giubilini and Minerva note that one third of all cases of Down's Syndrome were not discovered through pre-birth testing:

> This percentage indicates that, considering only the European areas under examination, about 1700 infants were born with Down's syndrome without parents being aware of it before birth. Once these children are born, there is no choice for the parents but to keep the child

Giubilini and Minerva speculate that a large number of parents whose baby is born with Down's Syndrome would have performed an abortion, had the condition been diagnosed during the pregnancy.

Then, government enters the picture:

> Nonetheless, to bring up such children might be an unbearable burden on the family and on society as a whole, when the state economically provides for their care.

At this point, it is no longer possible to keep the term "eugenics" out of the picture, nor is it possible to separate the term from the welfare state:

a) Government provides health care for "such children" based on egalitarian principles;
b) Tax revenue is scarce;
c) Therefore, government has to determine whose needs are worthy, and whose needs are unworthy, of being satisfied.

Since the rationing of needs is a direct result of the reconfiguration of society according to egalitarian principles, the decision to not satisfy a person's needs is a direct consequence of the ranking of the collective goal over the needs of the individual. Government seizes control over the individual's needs, puts them on equal footing and then – under the pressure of rationing – is forced to hierarchically exclude some individuals.

The decision whom to exclude is made based on a cost function attached to the person's utility function. Since rationing, according to the egalitarian playbook, is the consequence of an imbalance between tax revenue and spending on entitlements, it is logical to rank some people's needs above others until the budget deficit is gone.

Individuals whose needs end up too far down the list to be cared for, are ranked low because of a combination between the characteristics of their needs and the cost of satisfying those needs. Those individuals whose needs are less costly to satisfy, end up high on the list; those with higher-cost needs end up further down. The higher the cost to government – in other words to the welfare state – of a person's needs, the more likely it is that the person's needs will go uncared for.

According to Giubilini and Minerva, a child with Down's Syndrome is a net cost, an "unbearable burden" to government and therefore lives a life unworthy of living.

When individuals are discarded based on government budgetary considerations, an ideological goal, defining government spending, supersedes the right of an individual to live; since the superior goal of government is fiscal in nature, not racial, then this is a case of fiscal eugenics.

Lives unworthy of the welfare state

An important element of the welfare state is that government usurps authority over the needs of individuals. Not only does government thereby promise to satisfy those needs, but it also claims jurisdiction over those needs for the purposes of resource rationing.

The first purpose of rationing is to close a gap between existing needs and the needs that fit the government budget. If this were the only purpose, then the logical method to ration a scarce government resource – such as health care under a single-payer system – would be to randomly select a sufficient number of people whose needs will go unmet. That, however, is not how rationing is done; when entitlement programs fall short of providing for everyone eligible, the sorting mechanism tends to be tied to the resource shortfall itself. In other words, government uses the rationing method as part of a strategy to reduce, and eventually eliminate, excess demand.

Nowhere is this rationing method more conspicuously applied than in health care. Referring back to the medical ethics issue just discussed: if a baby is born with medical conditions that are serious enough to reduce or eliminate his ability to provide for himself as an adult, then the welfare state's sorting mechanism will rank his needs too low to satisfy. By the ethical standards proposed by Giubilini and Minerva, this means that government would permit a so called post-birth abortion.

There are real-life examples from government-run health care that come close to this sorting mechanism. In December 2012 the British newspaper the *Daily Mail* reported that, annually, as many as 60,000 patients die in the so-called Liverpool Care Pathway – a palliative-care system under the National Health Service – without having given prior consent to the withdrawal of life-sustaining treatment. In a third of the cases, family members are "kept in the dark" about treatment withdrawal.

The newspaper gave a detailed account of what treatment withdrawal actually meant:[7]

> The pathway involves withdrawal of lifesaving treatment, with the sick sedated and usually denied nutrition and fluids. Death typically takes place within 29 hours.

In other words, patients whose lives are deemed unaffordable are left to starve and dehydrate to death over a period longer than a day. The *Daily Mail* also reported some troubling facts from a study by the Marie Curie Palliative Care Institute and the Royal College of Physicians:

- Many patients are conscious when treatment is withdrawn, yet are not asked about whether or not they want to die.
- Thousands of patients were left to die without medication for pain.
- Financial incentives appear to promote hospitals and health trusts to put patients on the Liverpool Care Pathway.

In another article, from November 2012, the *Daily Mail* reported that children were also being put on the same path to death. That article, which remains widely quoted by many organizations and blogs on the internet, has been removed from the *Daily Mail*'s archive. However, on November 29, 2012, the *Daily Telegraph* reported that the Liverpool Care Pathway is indeed being applied to children and babies born with severe disabilities.[8] Concerns that parents are being persuaded, even coerced, into putting their children on this medical death row

> came as a doctor disclosed in a leading medical journal that he had presided over ten cases involving end-of-life procedures for newborns. In the article he described in excruciating detail how the process of withdrawing food and fluid from severely disabled newborns could take an average of ten days during which the infant becomes "smaller and shrunken."

The practice of starving and dehydrating a baby to death over ten days is part of a rationing process where government has jurisdiction over people's health-care needs. By virtue of that jurisdiction, government sorts lives worthy of saving from lives unworthy of the government budget. In the case of lives selected for termination, the premise is that they will not be able to deliver enough tax revenue over their life to compensate government for the cost of their treatment.

In some instances, such as the British National Health Service, a shortage of hospital beds plays a role in the fiscal calculation. The cost of adding and staffing more hospital beds goes into the live-or-die calculation: if government cannot expect to receive enough tax revenue, over the span of the patient's remaining life, to cover both treatment and the extra cost of adding hospital beds, then the patient will be discarded.

Calculations of fiscal eugenics do not only place infants with unaffordable medical conditions on the euthanasian "pathway," and not just in Britain. There is established academic support for using euthanasia to discard fiscally unfit individuals from the population. In a 1998 article for the *New England Journal of Medicine*, Harvard Medical School associate professor Ezekiel Emanuel and University of Utah philosophy professor Margaret Battin estimated cost savings from "physician-assisted suicide," also known as euthanasia. Their findings, reported in their article (Tables 1 and 2 on pages 169 and 170, respectively) suggest that for cancer patients, with health-care costs at average Medicare rates, savings would rate from $916 million to $1.6 billion in conventional care, and $490 million to $1.1 billion in hospice care.

These numbers are updated by GDP price indexes from the article's 1995 prices. Health-care costs have increased much faster; adjusting specifically for health-care inflation, the cost savings would run all the way up to $2.1 billion.

As noted by Emanuel and Battin, these are small numbers compared to total health-care expenditure in the United States. However, they are confined to cancer patients only, and based on the assumption that health-care costs are on par with Medicare costs. Under different institutional circumstances it is not only possible, but likely, that similar calculations would find cost savings to be many times greater.

Since 1998, the debate over euthanasia has slowly intensified and become normalized in the American conversation about health care. (This is ironic: death only terminates life; life itself is not a disease and euthanasia should logically not be part of the practice of medicine.) In 2013, four years after the passage of the Affordable Care Act, Robert Leeson, then Campbell National Fellow at the Hoover Institution of Stanford University, suggested that euthanasia can be "an economic decision made early." Trying to normalize euthanasia in an op-ed for the *San Francisco Chronicle*, the Hoover Institution fellow suggested that euthanasia inhibits the kind of rational choices that individuals make regarding "lifetime satisfaction." Moreover, Leeson explains:[9]

> many dying people are beyond the stage where they can act according to this calculation; younger people are much better equipped to make this rational choice in advance. At the beginning and the end of a working life, individuals should be free to decide about such matters.

Leeson goes on to suggest that young people should buy a kind of health insurance that would pay for their treatment during the diffuse period referred to as "end of life." He even suggests that such insurance purchases could be done against a

Medicare tax deduction, creating a direct link between government's cost for "end-of-life" treatment and the same government's right to pull the plug on patients it pays for. If a person buys "end-of-life" insurance, it will function as a bail-out of government's live-or-die decision-making process.

To make sure as many people as possible buy his proposed insurance, Leeson suggests that young people get it as soon as they enter the workforce. His motivation connects his proposal for managing the costs of government-funded health care to fiscal eugenics – consider the last sentence in this quote (emphasis added):

> Even if some final-year expenditures produce measurable benefits, these have to be weighed against alternative uses. There can be no objection to someone choosing to self-fund palliative care; *neither can there be an objection to the taxpayer choosing to fund, for example, better infant mortality outcomes than end-of-life expenses.*

In this line of thinking, where life itself is a cost item, Hoover Institution fellow Robert Leeson applies the same kind of egalitarianism and fiscal eugenics as the Myrdals stipulated in their 1934 book *The Demographic Crisis*. The moral hierarchy is the same, with the needs of the state – here represented by "the taxpayer" – superseding the needs of the individual. Leeson's logic is the exact same as the logic where the British government slots some babies for starvation to death. Government has jurisdiction over the individual's needs, and therefore has the authority to instrumentally sort between those needs.

It is noteworthy that Leeson accepts the demotion of life itself before questioning whether or not government should provide for needs that it cannot satisfy. In his acceptance lies the axiomatic acknowledgment of a government-run health-care system; in plain English, Leeson sees the reasons for allowing government to run and ration health care as having higher moral value than life itself.

He is far from alone. Health-care economists have developed sophisticated methods for making life-or-death calculations, methods that are being applied in single-payer health-care systems in, for example, Britain and Sweden. The best-known method is known by its acronym QALY, which stands for Quality Adjusted Life Years. It was developed in the 1960s and is applied in government-run health-care systems in many countries, though not in the United States.[10] It is a system that weighs two levels of costs and benefits:

- the cost of providing a medical procedure against the patient's expected health benefits; and
- the cost to government of the patient's improved health against the taxes that the individual can be expected to pay in the future.

Few countries match Sweden in the implementation of egalitarian policies, and of QALY in its health-care system. As reported in Larson (2010), Swedish health care is subject to serious rationing problems, claiming lives of thousands of patients per year that would have survived had they been given proper, available treatment. Yet because of rationing they died.

Swedish health care, a single-payer system since the 1950s, is a prime example of egalitarian-driven rationing. The private health insurance and health-care options that do exist were either grandfathered in when health care was socialized in the 1950s, or have popped up in a marginal, regulatory gray zone in response to serious access and quality problems in the government-run health system.[11]

The system is closely guided by centralized rules for resource allocation. Under guidelines from the National Board of Health and Welfare (*Socialstyrelsen*) all health-care providers apply QALY calculations when distributing rationed health care among patients. In a 2011 report on cost assessment for preventative medicine, the National Board of Health and Welfare defined four levels of QALY analysis outcomes. Benefits of providing health care can be low, moderate, high or very high; given the patient's health and outlook on life, the higher the QALY benefit, the more likely the medical procedure will be provided.[12] Conversely, if the QALY score is low enough, the patient is denied the procedure.

For all its technical sophistication, the QALY method is one of the best representations of the egalitarian moral hierarchy. In order to perform a QALY calculation, government needs to attach a value to the patient's improved health. That is done by standardized assessments, detached from the patient himself. It is not the patient who decides how much his improved health is worth to him – that decision is made by a government official based on what government deems his improved health is worth.

A standard method for ascribing a value to health improvement is to give it a number in the 0–1 interval, with 0 representing death and 1 being equal to perfect health. When calculating the QALY for providing a patient with a given medical procedure, a government employee plugs a health improvement value into the model. Based on that value, and all other variables included, the model provides a QALY value, upon which a government employee – ostensibly a physician – decides whether or not the patient should be treated.

Sweden has found another area for QALY calculations, namely the country's government-run, monopolized supply of prescription medicine. While private competition is permitted at the retail level, government maintains a strict wholesale monopoly on pharmaceutical products. One of the roles of that monopoly is to bulk buy medicine at pre-negotiated prices. The application of QALY in this system is described in detail in a November 2012 seminar briefing by the British Office of Health Economics. Ulf Persson, author of the briefing, is a Swedish health-care economist and member of the board of the government agency that runs the pricing system for the country's drug supply.[13]

With the technical clarity of an engineer's diary, Persson explains the core principles that underpin the Swedish value-based pricing (VBP) method for pharmaceutical products. The first and foremost pricing guideline is the "social and economic perspective" on "the impact of using new treatments on the broader economy and society" of a patient being, or not being, treated with a new drug. This is, Persson writes, the "first, and most important, focus of the Swedish VPB system."

Then the calculation takes a turn into the shadow realm of fiscal eugenics:

> A human capital approach is used to calculate production loses [*sic*] due to absence of early retirement because of illness. When treatment prolongs life, we consider the costs for life-years gained, which are equal to total consumption less total production during those additional years.

Here is what a plain-English version of this paragraph would sound like:

> When we decide whether or not a new medical drug is worth the government's money, we look at how often the sick person will be away from work if he does not get treated. That gives us an idea of how much or how little he will be paying in taxes for the rest of his life. If the drug works and he lives longer than he would have without it, we estimate the cost of the drug vs. what taxes he will be paying during those extra years we give him. If we think he will pay more in taxes than it cost to give him the treatment, then sure, let him have the drug. If his expected future tax payments won't cover treatment costs, then government sees no reason why he should have the medicine.

The government agency for whom Ulf Persson is speaking, does not get involved in individual prescriptions of medicine. Instead, it makes this kind of eugenic decisions at the macro level, calculating whether or not the average patient in need of a specific drug will make a tax profit for government over the rest of his life. If the agency finds that the average, standardized patient will produce a tax profit for government, then the drug is put on the government's list of tax-reimbursed drugs. If the average patient will cost more than he will contribute, the drug does not make the list. (A drug that does not make the list will not be accessible to patients in Swedish health care.)

Let us put this policy in perspective of the demographic goals that Gunnar and Alva Myrdal outlined in their 1934 book *The Demographic Crisis*. The very goal with their "prophylactic social policy" was to improve what they referred to as the "population stock" in order to maximize its labor-force performance. This, in turn, was necessary to provide the private sector with the best possible workers – and thereby guarantee a production value that would maximize tax revenue.

According to the Myrdals, only if tax revenue were maximized would government be able to keep all its spending promises. While it was fairly easy for governments in both Europe and North America to balance their budgets when welfare states were young, that has not been the case for at least three decades now. Therefore, welfare-state governments add rationing systems to more and more of their entitlement programs. Health care is the most obvious of them, in part because of its exceptional costs and in part because it is a morally charged type of service.

When welfare-state governments realize that they have to be systematic about rationing, their premise for doing so is not to put the patient above the health-care system. That would mean a complete overhaul and return to a system with private funding and delivery. Instead, the moral principle that guided the socialization of health care in the first place is now used as a schematic for designing rationing methods. The difference is that this time, the system is not guided by the first principle of egalitarianism – eradication of differences in outcomes – but by the second principle: maximize tax revenue to minimize rationing.

Just as the Myrdals advocated forced sterilization and other measures to discard costly or unproductive individuals from the population stock, the QALY method for rationing medicines in the Swedish health-care system denies treatment to people whose productivity in terms of tax revenue does not measure up to what government needs. As if to put this point in bold text, Ulf Persson goes into detail explaining how cost efficient their QALY-guided Value Based Pricing system is: the more medical drugs that his government entity rejects, the more effective the government agency is in controlling the costs of medicines in Sweden.[14]

The more restrictive the Swedish government is in approving new medicines, the more money it saves in terms of having to treat unproductive citizens. Patients whose future is going to be a net cost to government are selected.

Sweden is not alone in applying fiscal eugenics to its health-care system. In Britain, where some 95 percent of the entire population is subject to government-provided medicine, the National Institute for Health and Clinical Excellence (NICE) applies QALYs for the same rationing purposes as they are applied in Sweden. In a report on the British health-care rationing system, Public Radio International provides a good layman's explanation of how QALY works.[15] In a nutshell, here is how it is practiced:

- Suppose Jack and Joe have the same cancer and can receive the same life-extending cancer treatment at the cost of $100,000.
- Both Jack and Joe would live an extra four years from the treatment, putting the annual cost of the treatment at $25,000 per patient.
- Jack is expected to be in pain half the time during his four extra years, reducing life quality by half.
- Joe, on the other hand, will have no pain during his extra four years.
- If government chooses to treat Jack, it will only get $50,000 worth of "quality life" out of the treatment, whereas Joe would enjoy $100,000 worth of "quality life" for the same money.

As Public Radio International reports, these calculations are not just some abstract fiscal model. They are very much reality. The British National Institute for Health and Clinical Excellence (NICE)

> has set a maximum that it will spend on a treatment: about $47,000 per quality-adjusted year gained.... [NICE] has calculated that some of the more

> expensive drugs meant to slow the progression of Alzheimer's Disease and some cancers fall below the cost-effectiveness threshold. In such cases, NICE says, the NHS shouldn't pay for the drugs.

According to the same article, NICE chairman Michael Rawlins admits that unless end-of-life treatment is scaled back, Britain might see less money being spent "at the beginning of life" and, as a result, an increase in infant mortality.

Rather than permitting a health-care system where every patient would be in charge of his own health destiny, without having to have his cost effectiveness compared to others, the British government – like its Swedish counterpart – prefers to maintain the egalitarian institution of socialized health care. Rather than ranking the individual as morally superior to the collective, the British and Swedish governments prefer to rank the collective as morally superior to the individual.

It is problematic enough for friends of egalitarianism that the health-care system, when organized according to their ideology, deliberately deprives individuals of the remainder of their lives for the very purpose of preserving the ideological project. But the egalitarian case gets even weaker when merciless evaluating light is placed on the performance – or lack thereof – of egalitarian-driven health-care systems. In December 2014, the New Jersey-based IMS Institute for Healthcare Informatics evaluated the impact of QALY-based rationing models in five countries: Australia, Canada, England, Scotland and Sweden. Those countries were then compared to five countries that did not apply QALY-based rationing methods: France, Germany, Italy, Spain and the United States.[16]

Focus was specifically on the access to cancer drugs; they reported that on the one hand, costs for cancer drugs per new patient was clearly lower in countries that apply QALY-based rationing. On the other hand, in QALY-rationing countries (Aitken 2014: 7):

- Patients "have less access to new cancer drugs";
- There are "fewer new cancer drugs" on reimbursement lists (and therefore de facto not available) and drugs that are approved are delayed by long approval processes;
- Those drugs that reach patients are prescribed more restrictively;
- Patients are less likely to survive cancer; and
- The cost of health care is not necessarily lower, but the health care system "may achieve less for patients."

In short, egalitarianism asks people to surrender their sacrosanct right to life, subordinate themselves to government policies and if necessary be ready to die prematurely, all in order to preserve the welfare state or contain its economic shortcomings. Or, in the words of Jane M Orient, executive director of the Association of American Physicians and Surgeons:[17]

> there is an unbridgeable chasm between life and death. Nevertheless, the discontinuity apparently escapes those who set up relative value scales based on "quality-adjusted life-years" (QALYs). The unstated assumption is that at some point on the QALY scale, visible to experts, the value of a life becomes negative – even less than the value of death.

The question that egalitarians need to answer, in order to save their welfare state for the foreseeable future, is whether or not the demotion of life to an instrument for egalitarianism – in other words economic redistribution – is a moral price they are willing to pay. If the answer is yes, under what other entitlement programs are they willing to demote life to an instrument for ideological purposes?

Notes

1 Nozick (1974).
2 Sewell (2009).
3 Spektorowski and Mizrachi (2004).
4 Pierson-Balik (2003).
5 Osborn (1937).
6 Giubilini and Minerva (2013).
7 See www.dailymail.co.uk/news/article-2255054/60-000/patients-death-pathway-told-minister-says-controversial-end-life-plan-fantastic.html (accessed May 18, 2017).
8 See www.telegraph.co.uk/news/health/news/9710426/Children-placed-on-controversial-death-pathway.html (accessed May 18, 2017).
9 See www.sfgate.com/opinion/article/Euthanasia-can-be-an-economic-decision-made-early-4888933.php (accessed May 18, 2017).
10 Some argue for the introduction of the QALY method into American health care. For example: Neumann and Greenberg (2009).
11 The only private provision of health care that is legally permitted is confined to general-practice health-care clinics. Government maintains tight control over private providers by means of funding – private payment and private insurance is almost entirely illegal – and through an elaborate certificate-of-need process.
12 See www.socialstyrelsen.se/nationellariktlinjerforsjukdomsforebyggandemetoder/Documents/nr-sjukdomsforebyggande-halsoekonomisktunderlag.pdf (accessed May 18, 2017).
13 Persson (2012).
14 See Tables 1 and 2 in the report. Table 2 reports the percentage of applications from pharmaceutical companies that the government agency approves or denies. Table 1 reports the annual rise in costs for pharmaceuticals in Sweden. A comparison of the two tables reveals that with a one-year lag, restrictive government approval of new drugs is reflected in slow cost increases, and vice versa. In other words, when government works hard to deny access to new pharmaceutical products, the cost of treating people's serious medical conditions is kept under tabs.
15 See www.pri.org/stories/2010-12-17/how-uk-rations-health-care (accessed May 18, 2017).
16 Aitken (2014).
17 Orient (2006).

6

PROBLEM 2

Slow Growth

Over the past 15–30 years, depending on country, welfare states have experienced a sustained decline in economic growth. The decline started in Europe, in some instances as early as in the late 1970s, and formed a trend during the late 1980s and 1990s. The U.S. economy did not see the same decline until after the Millennium Recession, but the European trend nevertheless made it across the Atlantic Ocean.

Economists will always debate the causes of changes in long-term macroeconomic trends, and that debate is necessary. That said, there is also a tendency among economists to over-complicate issues, especially by over-reliance on rigorous quantitative methods (also known as econometrics). Those methods are not always capable of capturing major economic trends, primarily because the study of such trends cannot always be given the analytical "side boards" econometricians need.

Therefore, it is sometimes necessary to rely on more basic, yet established economic theory and experience. The long-term decline in growth in our welfare states is a good example. In other words, consider the following stylized facts:

- A welfare state socializes large sectors of the economy, putting the production of services under government monopoly.
- Because of its monopolistic position, government is inferior to the private sector in producing low-cost, high-quality services.
- As a result of large-scale monopolization (education, health care, child care, income security), government slows down growth in a substantial slice of the economy.
- The more elaborate the welfare state becomes, the higher the taxes it needs to pay for its promises.
- High taxes discourage productive private-sector activity.

Based on this reasoning it is fair to conclude that the long-term decline in growth in the world's highest-taxed economies is primarily the result of the expansion of the welfare states themselves.[1] However, regardless of whether proponents of the welfare state accept these stylized facts, they have an inescapable problem before them. When the welfare states of the Western world have to rely on slow-to-no growth in their tax bases, while demand for their entitlement programs continues to increase, it inevitably leads to a fundamental conflict between egalitarian ambitions and economic reality.

The tension between those ambitions and slow growth is the second problem that friends of the welfare state must address, should they wish to save the egalitarian project for the future.

The Swedish experience

Sweden was able to combine the completion of a full-scale welfare state with high growth rates all the way through the 1960s (see Figure 6.1).

The RM economic-policy model was a major factor behind the growth success. Its promotion of exports helped the economy sustain growth even as gradually rising taxes began taking a toll on domestic demand. Furthermore, the Swedish economy benefited from centralization of home construction, which was integrated

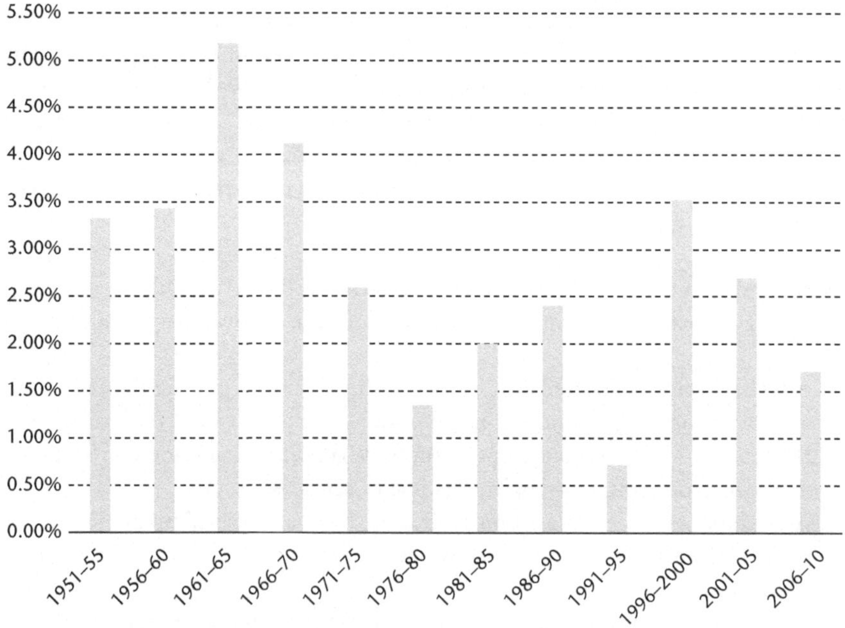

FIGURE 6.1 GDP, Sweden: fixed prices, domestic currency

Source: United Nations National Accounts Database

into large-scale economic and geographic planning. Infrastructure expansion was combined with assembly-line style construction of entire suburbs of housing projects; government-run services were expanded and woven into those communities, forming master-planned local societies. Worker migration was encouraged, even forced, by the "solidarity in wages" policies under the RM model.

The 1950s saw the institutional completion of the Swedish welfare state; the 1960s was the decade of socio-economic master planning, physically reconfiguring society to the needs and demands of the egalitarian political project. The population clustered where the multi-national corporations were, sending their children to schools that were fully standardized under one national curriculum. Their health needs were taken care of by health clinics and hospitals, all run by government and funded by income taxes. They no longer had to worry about income security, either short term while on leave from work, or long term when retiring.

Gunnar Myrdal predicted that a centrally planned welfare state, with all its economic-policy add-ons, would thrive off high, sustained growth rates for the foreseeable future. He also predicted that the Swedish economy would be able to do this despite the high taxes needed to fund the welfare state.

Eventually, reality proved his prediction wrong, though not about taxes. The combined local and regional income tax, which paid for the bulk of services delivered by the welfare state, started increasing as soon as the welfare state was fully expanded. While varying regionally, the national average rate floated steadily around 10.5 percent from 1931 through 1955. After that, it only went up: to 17.3 percent in 1965, 25.2 percent in 1975 and 30.4 percent in 1985.

Together with value-added tax and a national payroll tax, local and national income taxes paid the bulk of total tax revenue. The total tax burden on the Swedish economy began accelerating in the latter half of the 1960s and continued to rise through the 1980s, when it capped out at 50 percent (see Figure 6.2).

Once taxes began rising annually, GDP growth declined:[2]

TABLE 6.1 Growth and tax burden

	1966–1970	*1976–1980*
Average annual tax burden	34%	44%
Average annual GDP growth	4.1%	1.4%

As a general observation, when the combined tax burden on an economy adds up to 40 percent of GDP, it seems to cause a permanent downshift in economic growth. There is a fair amount of research to support the 40 percent mark as a breaking point for GDP growth (Afonso *et al.* 2005; Gill and Raiser 2012; Larson 2014, Chapter 3). Most European welfare states passed that mark in the 1970s, and consequently have struggled to keep their economies growing at rates that can feed their welfare states.

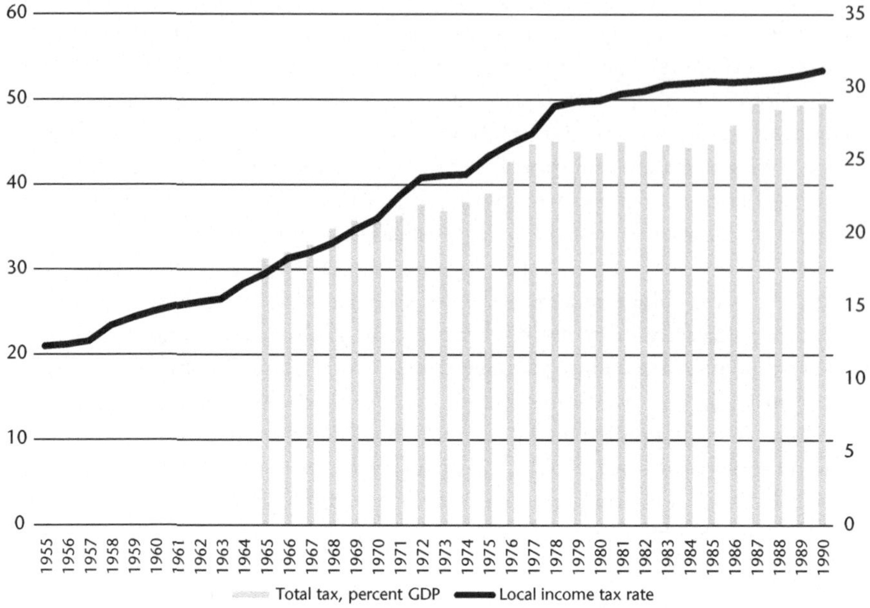

FIGURE 6.2 Sweden: local income tax rates (right axis); total tax burden on GDP (left axis)

Source: Statistics Sweden (scb.se) for income tax rates; OECD (oecd.org) for total burden as percent of GDP. The tax burden is calculated based on current-price GDP, measured in US dollars

However, even if the statistical facts are indisputable; even if the decline in growth undeniably coincides with welfare-state expansion past the 40 percent mark; the academic literature is rife with arguments suggesting that the welfare state is not entirely to blame.

Defending the welfare state in a slow-growth economy

Behind the resistance to regarding the welfare state as responsible for causing slow growth is a theory that, in the academic literature, has been named the "exogenous theory" of the welfare state. It suggests that the welfare state's only contributions to society and the economy are positive in nature. Its widespread support suggests that Gunnar Myrdal was right in his prediction in 1958 that the welfare state would soon enjoy universal support, or its opponents would perish from the public spotlight.

Up until the last quarter of the twentieth century, egalitarians did not have to work very hard to defend the welfare state. It seemed to stand on its own merits. Yet as the twentieth century drew to a close, the "new normal" of low GDP growth and persistent budget deficits made it impossible to continually finance, let alone expand the welfare state. Pressured by tighter streams of revenue, governments all over Europe had to focus more on increasingly tougher budget priorities.

Conventional wisdom among academic scholars declared the welfare state innocent in its own revenue dry-up. However, the fiscal-sustainability problems became so prevalent that it could no longer be ignored. A pursuit began, primarily among scholars leaning in the egalitarian direction, for an answer to what role – if any – the welfare state really played in Europe's growth slowdown.

Exogenous theorists, as well as egalitarian political practitioners, have been remarkably resilient in making their case that the welfare state has no negative impact on the economy. While the economics profession for the most part has shied away from this political-economy topic,[3] egalitarians have found support in some contributions from practitioners of the dismal science. Foremost among them is John Kenneth Galbraith, whose long line of work firmly suggests that he believed the welfare state to be only, or predominantly, a positive contribution to the economy.

More recently, scholars inspired by the fiscal stress on Europe's welfare states overwhelmingly base their work on the exogenous theory. This theory has, so to speak, become the prevailing wisdom in welfare-state research. There is general agreement in the literature that, on the balance, the legislative success of egalitarianism has been good for society and the economy.

Inevitably, this conclusion must suggest that the welfare state is innocent in the case of declining GDP growth. There are two ways to make this case: either by the suggestion that the growth slowdown has other causes; or by proposing that the welfare state does not need strong growth to prevail.

The first strategy requires theoretically and methodologically complex analysis. It demands the identification of a global economic phenomenon capable of pulling all welfare states down toward economic stagnation during the same period of time. Furthermore, it necessitates the refutation of basic microeconomic theory, such as the negative reaction of economic agents to higher taxes. So far, no such case has been convincingly presented, though James Galbraith (2012), focused on the Great Recession and its aftermath, is a challenging yet isolated exception.

In lieu of solid support by means of the first strategy, proponents of the exogenous theory of the welfare state have resorted to the second strategy. Joel Blau, professor of social welfare and policy at Stony Brook University, is at the frontline of the no-growth-is-good-news argument. In a 1989 article for *Social Service Review* he notes that the decline in growth in Western economies in the 1970s and 1980s did not put an end to welfare-state growth. Therefore (pp. 26–27):

> As the social costs of a minimalist state have become more apparent in the late 1980s, the conservative view of the welfare state has lost its power, and there are signs we are approaching the threshold of a new conception that calls for increased public responsibility.

Blau actually defines the exogenous welfare state so that when continuous growth in spending correlates with stagnant GDP growth, it is evidence that the welfare state is a success. That point aside, his metrics define the American welfare state as a success. Essentially, the argument goes as follows: over the past two decades Social Security spending has grown by 5 percent per year, while other entitlement spending has grown by 6–8 percent per year.[4] In the same amount of time, GDP growth has declined by about one percentage point. By Blau's metrics and the exogenous theory, this means that the American welfare state is successful because it survives in a stagnant economy.

Blau provides an insight into how egalitarians address the issue of sluggish growth based on the exogenous theory. The generalized point is that the welfare state can survive regardless of how quickly, or how slowly, the economy is growing. This point is not without support in the literature. In 1994, Swedish economist Torsten Persson and his Italian colleague Guido Tabellini suggested that large economic differences between citizens led to "distributional conflict," in response to which "political decisions produce economic policies that tax investment and growth-promoting activities in order to redistribute income."[5]

In other words, when politicians are guided by egalitarianism, they will disregard growth in their quest to reduce or eliminate economic differences. Growth is no longer essential to the welfare state as it was to Gunnar Myrdal and John Galbraith; it is irrelevant. Focus shifted from growth to economic redistribution, although persistent problems with slow growth and budget deficits have fueled an ongoing debate over the relationship between redistribution and growth. During the 1990s, there was a surge in academic research suggesting that the larger the income differences are in a country, the weaker its growth will be.

Interestingly, in 1994, the same year as Persson and Tabellini conclude that large economic differences are negative for the economy, Persson himself contributed to the conclusion that larger income differences are necessary to increase growth in the Swedish economy.[6]

He is not the only one to contend that the pursuit of economic redistribution can be economically harmful. In 2000, MIT economist Kristin Forbes took on the research that concluded in favor of economic redistribution. She criticized their statistical work, concluding that they made too many hens out of one feather. She presented results that "clearly challenge the current belief that income inequality has a negative effect on economic growth."[7]

In 2003, three OECD researchers summarized the economic theory that says inequality can actually be good for growth:[8]

> in a closed economy, the greater the savings, the lower the cost of capital and the greater the rate of investment, hence … the greater the rate of growth. Because the rich have a higher savings ratio than the poor, it follows that the more unequally national income is distributed, the greater will be the aggregate savings rate, and hence the greater will be the investment and growth rate. Income redistribution would retard growth unless governments took additional steps to ensure that investment remained high.

There was also a broader theoretical effort to counter the egalitarian arguments. One of the leading economists was Art Laffer, best known for the Laffer curve and his contributions to President Reagan's sweeping tax-cut reforms. However, the most interesting part of Laffer's contributions is in a point he made about the welfare state that egalitarians have only countered with great difficulty. Lower taxes, Laffer pointed out repeatedly (and correctly), generate more growth. The opposite is, of course, true as well.

American stagnation

The U.S. economy left the twentieth century with growth in excess of 4 percent, only to plunge into a long period of slow growth. For every year that is added to the twenty-first century, growth peaks in excess of 3 percent become fewer and farther in between, with the Obama presidency closing its macroeconomic record without a single year of 3 percent of GDP growth.

Only two decades ago, egalitarians would not hesitate to capitalize on the 4+ percent growth rates during President Clinton's second term. Now, America's welfare statists appear to have abandoned the pursuit of strong growth. A fast-growing economy is no longer a sign of success. Consistent with the exogenous theory of the welfare state, present-day egalitarians consider the growth issue as something between irrelevant and a distraction.

In this way, the American left has come a long way from the days of President Kennedy and his growth-promoting policies. Where President Kennedy, even President Johnson despite his egalitarian leaning, were favorable to a "compassionate" balance between the free market and the social state, today's American left is not satisfied with a government that spends seven times more on income redistribution than it does on national defense. Increasingly, the Democratic Party has become dedicated to creating a full-scale American version of the Scandinavian welfare state.

It is easy to find examples of how the American left has demoted the pursuit of economic growth to, at best, a second-tier goal, while relentlessly committing to more economic redistribution. A forefront representative of this view is former presidential candidate and Senator Bernie Sanders (D-VT). During the 2016 presidential race he vocally and repeatedly advocated for reduced income differences while being equally explicit in his skepticism of economic growth. For example, in a quote from the *Washington Post*, July 2015, Sanders wanted an end to growth "for the sake of growth":

> we've got to move to a society that provides a high quality of life for all of our people. In other words, if people have health care as a right, … then there's less worry about growth. If people have educational opportunity and their kids can go to college and they have child care, then there's less worry about growth for the sake of growth.

The Institute for Policy Studies, the oldest progressive think tank in Washington, DC, went a step farther. In a 2013 article, American sociology professor Salvatore Babones suggested that income redistribution actually benefits economic growth – and that large income differences lead to slow growth. Hardly surprising, he recommends more policies to redistribute more income, and not worry about growth.[9]

Babones may not worry about the empirical evidence against his policy proposals, but some egalitarians are not so quick to dismiss the virtues of growth. Economist Heather Boushey is one of them. She is the executive director and chief economist at the Washington Center for Equitable Growth and was tapped in August 2016 as the chief economist of Hillary Clinton's presidential transition team. A lot of Boushey's research is focused on income differences and producing proposals for new entitlement programs. As for economic growth, her argument is clear: "In the long run" she suggests, "more equitable societies are associated with higher rates of growth."[10]

This is not at all the case. To escape the evidence against her suggestions, Boushey relies entirely on the questionable "long term" time frame. Swedish economist Assar Lindbeck has proven that "long term" is the span of a century;[11] unless Boushey has a different definition of long term hidden somewhere in the obscure corners of her own writings, her point about equitable societies and "high rates of growth" is completely void of any economic meaning.

Despite the empirical challenges for the no-growth argument, there is no shortage of plans for how to expand the American welfare state in our current slow-growth economy. Boushey, again, has for more than a decade advocated universal child care, funded and operated by the federal government.[12] She is also a strong advocate for so-called paid family leave, an entitlement program where government provides general income security to families. The idea is to tax people's income – for example in the form of a payroll tax – and pay them a benefit in the form of part of their income when they are away from work on sick leave, to care for their children or for any other reason eligible under the program.[13]

President Obama supported expanding the welfare state. According to the *New York Magazine*, in 2015 he

> cemented a decision by the Democratic Party to make quality universal child care the next major goal of American liberalism. Obama signaled his intention in the State of the Union address, when he announced, "it's time we stop treating child care as a side issue, or as a women's issue, and treat it like the national economic priority that it is for all of us."[14]

In a speech in Warren, Michigan, on August 11, 2016,[15] Democratic presidential candidate Hillary Clinton criticized "too much inequality" in America. She called for more social and economic upward mobility, suggesting that it is "just too hard to get ahead today." In July 2015 she declared her "fairness economy" doctrine, where she explained how she wants to add new entitlement programs to the American welfare state:[16]

> Fair pay and fair scheduling, paid family leave and earned sick days, childcare are essential to our competitiveness and our growth. And we can do this in a way that doesn't impose unfair burdens on businesses, especially small businesses.

After a token reference to the need for economic growth, she returned focus to her egalitarian ambition, explaining that income inequality is "a drag" on the economy. Secretary Clinton's use of this term is not unique: it is often associated with references to economic inequality with the implication that if income differences were smaller – or went away entirely – the economy would grow faster.

In April 2016 Clinton re-iterated her commitment to growing entitlements as a means for income redistribution. By then, some of her critics took the opportunity to counter her arguments, though they did so primarily not by countering her arguments, but by pointing to her expensive attire.[17] If anything, that remark symbolizes the ineptitude of conservatives in challenging the egalitarian agenda.

These ambitions to further expand government spending on economic redistribution deserve a context. Consider Figure 6.3 which reports the entitlement share of federal spending since World War II. In 1964, 34 cents of every dollar the federal government spent went toward an entitlement program of some kind. Even that number was historically high: in the first 20 years after World War II, from 1945 to 1964, the entitlement share of the budget averaged 27.6 percent.

Once the War on Poverty and its entitlement programs became a reality, entitlement spending accelerated like a Dodge Hellcat. At an average annual rate of 8.8 percent since 1964, entitlements consumed 40 percent of the federal budget in 1970. Only three years later the share exceeded 50 percent. After a relative slowdown during President Reagan, entitlement growth gathered speed again under President Clinton. It reached 60 percent in 1994 and two thirds in 2002.

In less than 40 years the entitlement share of the federal budget had doubled. By 2015 73 cents of every federal dollar was designated for income-redistributing entitlements (see Figure 6.3).

The dramatic expansion of entitlement spending has completely changed the priorities of the federal government:

- In 1964, for every dollar Congress spent on national defense and administration of justice, it spent $0.73 on entitlements.
- In 2015, for every dollar Congress spent on national defense and administration of justice, it spent $5.38 on entitlements.

In other words, there can be no doubt that egalitarianism has conquered the United States of America. However, that conquest comes at a price (see Figure 6.4).

In 1955–1964, the ten years immediately preceding the War on Poverty, GDP grew by, on average, 3.9 percent per year (adjusted for inflation); entitlement spending was 31.9 percent of the federal budget.

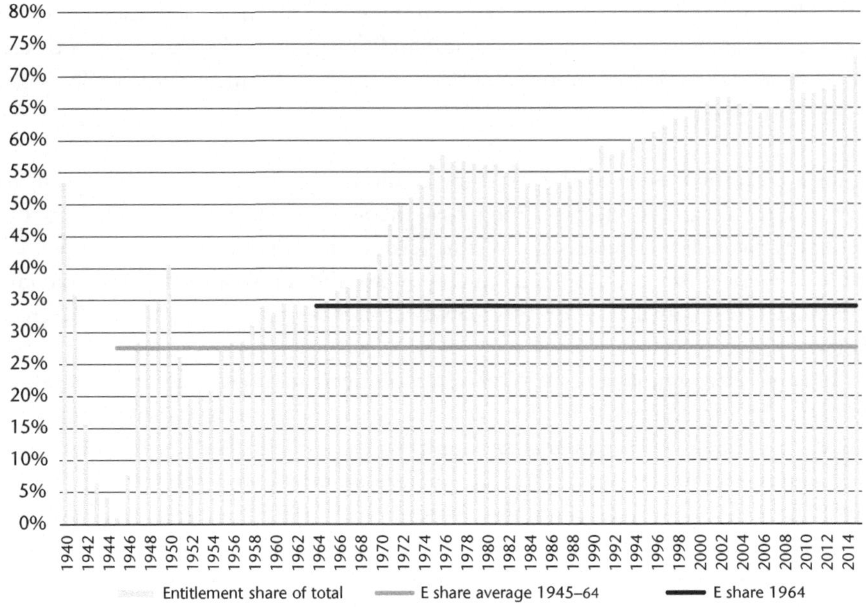

FIGURE 6.3 Entitlement share of federal spending

Source: Office of Management and Budget

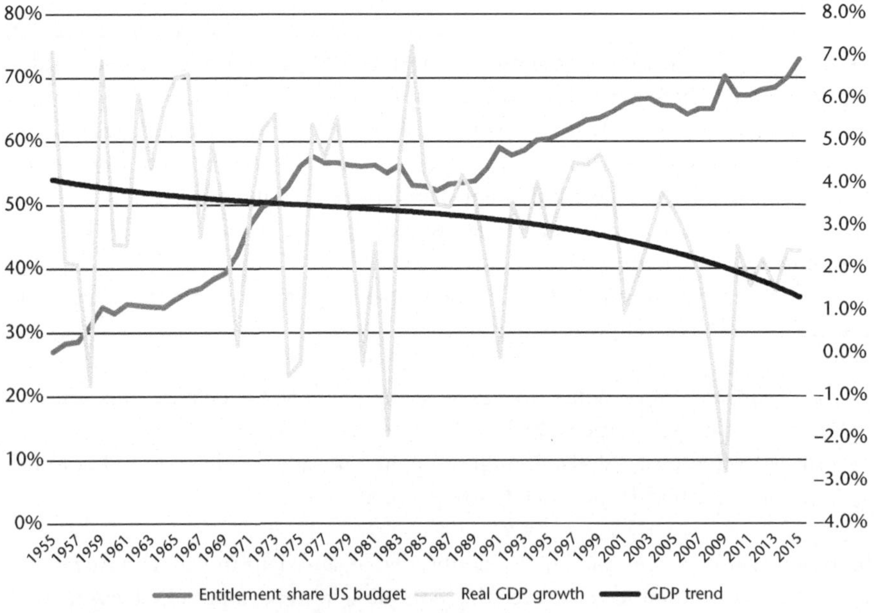

FIGURE 6.4 Real GDP growth: entitlement share of federal budget

Source: Office of Management and Budget (entitlements); Bureau of Economic Analysis (GDP growth)

In the following decades, as the federal government concentrated more and more of its spending on entitlements, annual GDP growth weakened, hovering marginally above 3 percent, and eventually dropped to depressing levels:

TABLE 6.2 Growth and entitlement shares

	GDP growth	*Entitlement share*
1965–1974	3.8%	42.9%
1975–1984	3.1%	56.0%
1985–1994	3.1%	55.7%
1995–2004	3.4%	64.0%
2005–2014	1.5%	67.1%

The past two years have not been much better for the U.S. economy: 2.4 percent in 2015 and (preliminarily) 1.2 percent in 2016.

Despite these numbers, America's egalitarians continue to advocate for more of their policies. Their intellectual lineage runs all the way back to John Kenneth Galbraith, who made no secret of the fact that he wanted the United States to adopt a full-scale version of a Scandinavian-style welfare state. As mentioned earlier, the left of the American political spectrum brims with proposals for further entitlement expansion.

Three angles on the growth problem: the EITC revisited

Given the grave consequences of long-term economic stagnation, it is imperative that welfare statists take notice of the evidence that the welfare state causes slow growth. In addition to what has been said thus far, the following sections present the same evidence from three different angles.

The first angle involves a more detailed look at the Earned Income Tax Credit (EITC), which combines, in concentrate, institutionalized egalitarianism and its growth-discouraging features.

Precisely because of the EITC's obviously egalitarian nature, one would expect some criticism of the entitlement program, at least from those who pledge allegiance to economic freedom and an entrepreneur-friendly economy. Sadly, outspoken critics of the EITC are few and far between.[18] It is all the easier for supporters of the program, even among those who, at least by affiliation, should have an inclination to be opposed to the idea of economic redistribution.

Michael Strain, director of economic-policy studies and resident scholar at the American Enterprise Institute (AEI), is a good example. In an article in the *Washington Post* on March 26, 2015, Strain made a passionate plea for an expansion of the Earned Income Tax Credit (EITC), suggesting that when the program had been expanded, the result was that "significant numbers" of people have left unemployment and joined the ranks of working Americans.[19] He also makes the not uncommon argument that the EITC is a tool for ending poverty, especially families with children whose maximum benefit is 12 times the maximum benefit for individuals with no children.

Strain then presents his policy prescription:

> The maximum EITC benefit for childless workers should be expanded. President Obama has proposed an expansion that would cost roughly $6 billion a year. Rep. Paul Ryan (R-Wis.) has a similar proposal.

As explained in Chapter 1, the EITC has strong negative marginal tax effects that discourage workforce participation except for what is necessary to qualify for the EITC itself. In case these points have not been heard in the hallways of the AEI, here is a more detailed presentation of how the EITC puts egalitarian, economic-redistribution principles to work, discouraging growth-promoting workforce participation in the bargain.

Suppose Ken and Barbie have two children and file taxes jointly as married. Together they make $30,000, on which they pay 10 percent on the first $18,450 and then 15 percent on the remaining $11,550. One day, Ken gets a promotion at work. His income goes up by $5,000. The IRS takes 15 percent of that extra five grand in taxes. This is the marginal tax effect on his last earned dollars, according to the income-tax rates for 2015, for a couple filing jointly as married:

TABLE 6.3 Barbie and Ken's tax table

Income from	*to*	*Tax rate*
$0	$18,450	10%
$18,451	$74,900	15%
$74,901	$151,200	25%
$151,201	$230,450	28%
$230,451	$411,500	33%
$411,501	$464,850	35%
$464,851	or more	39.6%

To make this example simple and to-the-point, suppose that Ken and Barbie live in a state with no state or local income tax. Before the promotion Ken and Barbie have $26,419 left after federal taxes. When Ken gets the raise, their total income after tax increases by $4,250, adding up to $30,669 in disposable income.

That is not bad. In fact, the 15-percent marginal tax is low enough to make it attractive for Ken to accept the promotion. Cheered on by Barbie, his hard work allows him to pursue higher incomes and a more comfortable life for him, Barbie and their children.

That is, before the welfare state strikes. Years ago, Ken and Barbie signed up for the Earned Income Tax Credit. Before Ken accepts his promotion, he and Barbie get an extra $4,201 in refundable tax credit. This adds on to their net-tax income from work, which again is $26,419. With the EITC added onto that, they have $30,620 to spend every year.

But wait a second. We just said that without the EITC, Ken's promotion would increase their after-tax income to $30,669. Does that mean that the EITC has already elevated their household budget to the same level as Ken would be able to do if he accepted the promotion?

Yes, that is exactly what it means. By adding a bit more than four grand to their annual budget,

- On the one hand, the EITC makes life more comfortable on a low $30,000 income;
- On the other hand, the EITC makes it financially pointless for Ken to accept the promotion.

This is the egalitarian philosophy at work in Ken's and Barbie's family budget. They are discouraged from depending on their own skills to feed their children and provide for themselves; by the same token, they are encouraged to remain in low-paying jobs.

To be fair, the EITC does not go away completely with the promotion. Ken and Barbie get to keep some of it. Here is how the numbers turn out should Ken accept the promotion.

Since the marginal income tax is 15 percent, Ken has to pay $750 in taxes on the extra $5,000 he would earn. His net income increase is $4,250. At the same time the EITC will drop, and quite dramatically, by $1,053. That is money that Ken and Barbie will lose if he accepts the promotion.

When the $750 in new federal income taxes is calculated against the $1,053 in lost EITC, Ken and Barbie find that their after-tax income will increase by $3,217 – a far cry from the $4,250 they would have kept from the raise if there had been no EITC in the first place.

Is it still worth it for Ken to take the new job, with its extra responsibilities? Maybe, or maybe not. The problem is that the decline in the EITC works like a tax increase on Ken's and Barbie's bottom line. While the formal income tax rate is 15 percent, the loss of some of the EITC effectively raises their marginal tax rate to 36 percent:

Income tax on the $5,000 raise	$750
Reduction in EITC	$1,053
Total increased tax burden	$1,803

… which is equal to 36 percent of the $5,000 raise. This is Ken's and Barbie's actual marginal income-tax rate.

By comparison, you have to make almost $465,000 before you face a marginal tax that steep. There is a reason for that: you do not have to be Art Laffer to realize that high marginal income taxes discourage people from putting in more hours at work, accepting promotions or even training to start a new career. Even though everyone is different and makes different choices in the same situation, we all have a "price." Some people are discouraged by 25 percent marginal taxes, others by 30 percent. For some, the marginal tax rate does not matter until government takes half or more of their last earned dollar. But at the end of the day, the higher the marginal income tax, the fewer of us will think it is worth the while to put in that extra effort.

For Ken and Barbie, the fact that there is practically no opposition to the EITC and other egalitarian entitlement programs means that they have to bear the burden of lifelong dependency on government. The EITC is perhaps the biggest building block of the entitlement obstacle that Ken has to climb in order to make financial sense of his promotion, but it is not the only one.

Medicaid is available in some states for families with two children and a total pre-tax income of $30,000 per year. This puts Ken and Barbie in the sweet spot where they qualify – but it also means that they will disqualify themselves if Ken accepts the promotion and their pre-tax income rises to $35,000. The cut-off point for his family's Medicaid eligibility is at $33,546.

Luckily, Ken's employer offers a health plan that he and his family can join. Before accepting the promotion Ken asks the human resources office how much he is now going to have to pay out of his own pocket for that health plan. Thanks to the EITC effect he and Barbie will only have $268 extra per month, so there is not much money to play with here before the promotion starts costing Ken and Barbie money, instead of adding to their bottom line.

According to the Kaiser Family Foundation, which tracks costs of health plans across the country, in 2015 the average employee contribution to a health plan they get through work was $392 per month.[20]

All of a sudden, it looks like Ken and Barbie will *lose* $124 per month if he accepts the promotion.

But we are not done yet. At $30,000 per year Ken and Barbie and their two children qualify for food stamps, or SNAP.[21] On average, an eligible family of four receives $459 per month to spend on SNAP-qualified groceries. With the tentative income increase Ken and Barbie will end up a little bit above the SNAP income limit – and lose that benefit, too.

What looked like a juicy $5,000 annual raise has suddenly turned into a loss of $583 per month – or $6,996 per year!

All the three entitlement programs that Ken and Barbie enjoy – the EITC, Medicaid and SNAP – are designed to permanently increase the purchasing power of low-earning households. In other words, they are all egalitarian entitlement programs, perfectly serving their purpose even as they keep Ken and Barbie trapped in low-paying jobs.

Three angles on the growth problem: income redistribution

Established economic theory explains why income redistribution has a depressing effect on growth. Work-free income weakens the need for workforce participation as it provides people with a higher purchasing power than they otherwise would receive. If they can only get the entitlements if they work – as is the case with the Earned Income Tax Credit – then the entitlements discourage them from putting in more hours and from pursuing promotions and other higher-paying jobs.

Progressive income taxes, a staple of income-redistribution policies, discourage workforce participation by making it prohibitively costly to increase one's hours or, again, climb the corporate ladder. Once the marginal tax rate rises above a certain level it will not be worth the money to spend more time away from one's family, friends and hobbies.

When workforce participation is discouraged, the economy grows more slowly. This effect comes mainly from the tax side: not only do high taxes discourage workforce participation and therefore deprive businesses of an essential production source, but they also take away money from people that they otherwise would have spent or invested.

Entitlements also contribute to slow economic growth by discouraging low-skilled workers from pursuing higher-paying jobs – and from starting businesses. Why spend 14 or 16 hours or more every day building a business when, at least to begin with, you can make just as much money on a low-paying job plus entitlements – or living off entitlements entirely?

It is not difficult to find data that validate this theoretical argument. The Gini coefficient is a good instrument for quantifying the effects of redistributive policies. It puts a number on how income is distributed between citizens:

- The number 1 represents the highest possible income concentration, which at least theoretically means that one person makes all the money and nobody else makes a penny; and
- The number 0 represents a completely egalitarian distribution of income.

Gini coefficients are reported in two forms. The first form measures income distribution under free-market conditions without the welfare state; the second form adds the effects of income-redistribution policies under the welfare state.

These two forms provide a good tool for measuring the extent to which income redistribution affects the economy. For example, in 2014 the free-market Gini coefficient for a certain European country was 0.531, but after income redistribution it fell to 0.277. Here is how to calculate the effect of income redistribution on the economy of this European country:

1. Subtract 0.277 from 0.531, resulting in a difference of 0.254;
2. Divide 0.254 by 0.531, or the value for market-based income distribution;
3. The product of the division is 47.8 percent.

This percentage value is called the *Gini effect*. Its practical meaning is that income-redistribution policies eliminate almost half – 47.8 percent to be exact – of the income differences in this particular European country.

According to the theoretical argument discussed above, a big Gini effect should be associated with low GDP growth. A review of a large set of data from Europe confirms this theory. Eurostat, the statistical agency of the European Union, reports Gini data from 31 countries over a period of ten years (2005–2014). When the Gini effect from these countries is compared with economic growth data – in other words changes to inflation-adjusted Gross Domestic Product – a very interesting picture emerges.

To allow a review, the data on the Gini effect and GDP growth is divided into five groups based on GDP growth. The observations that are coupled with the largest growth rates are collected in the first quintile. As the dark line shows, GDP growth in this quintile is, on average, 6.3 percent per year. At the same time, the Gini effect is 35.8 percent, the lowest for any of the quintiles:

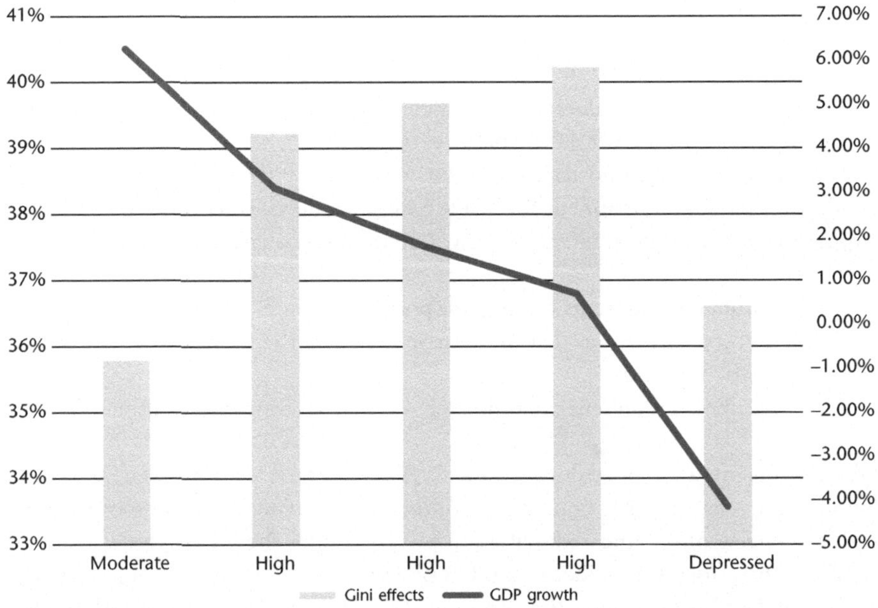

FIGURE 6.5 Gini effects: GDP growth

Source: Eurostat

The first quintile is labeled "moderate" to represent a moderate degree of income redistribution.

The next three quintiles represent "high" degrees of income redistribution: the average values of the Gini effects are, respectively, 39.2 percent, 39.7 percent and 40.2 percent. As the dark function explains, GDP growth clearly declines as the welfare state gets more ambitious in terms of income redistribution. For the three "high ambition" quintiles, the average growth rates are, from the left: 3.1 percent, 1.8 percent and 0.7 percent, respectively.

It is clear, then, that the more ambitious the welfare state is in altering free-market income distribution, the higher a price the economy will pay in the form of lower growth.

Figure 6.5 also reports an exception to this rule, namely the last quintile with the "depressed" label. Here the Gini effect is much lower again, only 36.6 percent. On the other hand, GDP growth is negative by a hefty –4.1 percent.

According to the theory that the other four quintiles confirm, this depressing level of growth should be associated with a skyrocketing Gini effect. Why is it not?

There is no simple answer to this question, but there is a plausible one. When GDP growth is negative, the economy is by definition in a recession; if negative growth persists over time the recession transitions into a depression. Regardless of whether the economy stays clear of a depression or not, a period of negative growth has two effects that can cause a reduction in the Gini effect.

The first effect is on employment. Recessions usually hit lower-income earners harder than people with higher salaries, the reason being that low-income jobs tend to be concentrated in businesses that are exposed to swings in the business cycle. As a result of the decline in income among low-wage earners, combined with relatively steady earnings higher up in the income hierarchy, the Gini effect declines. (Technically, the reason is that the Gini coefficient after income redistribution rises.)

The second effect is on tax revenue. An economy in trouble, with low or negative GDP growth, delivers insufficient tax revenue to the income-redistributing welfare state. This causes a budget deficit which, especially if sustained over time, forces cuts to income-redistributing entitlement programs. Furthermore, when governments raise taxes to fill a hole in their budgets they tend to raise them on a broad layer of taxpayers, rather than to concentrate the increases to high-income earners. There is, simply, not as much money to collect from wealthy citizens as there is from broad layers of moderate-to-middle income taxpayers.

As a result of cuts to entitlements and increases in taxes that primarily hit the middle class, the income-redistribution effect of the welfare state weakens. In Figure 6.5 this is displayed as a lower Gini effect.

Three angles on the growth problem: social expenditures

In his book *Inequality and Instability*, James Galbraith links the financial crisis of 2008 to economic differences (2012, p. 3):[22]

> The link, of course, runs through debt. For those with a little money, it is said, the spur of individuous comparison produces a want for more, and what cannot be earned must be borrowed. For those with little money to spare, made numerous by inequality and faced with exigent needs, there is also the ancient remedy of a loan. The urges and the needs, for bad or for good, are abetted by the aggressive desire of those with money to lend to those with less.

Credit, Galbraith points out, creates the illusion of an egalitarian standard of living, where families with low and moderate incomes can buy cars, homes, home electronics and other items at a standard they would otherwise not be able to afford. This has created an entire industry for household credit, both revolving (credit cards) and installment (mortgages, car loans).

At the other end of the transaction, high-income earners use the financial system to invest their savings. In the aggregate, wealthy households provide poor households with an opportunity to raise their standard of living without earning more. At the same time, Galbraith explains, this dependency on the financial system increases the instability of the economy. Unlike the real sector of the economy, the financial sector is prone to cumulative instability resulting in rapidly unfolding crises.

Galbraith links the credit-driven increase of low-income earners' standard of living to the episodes of instability. Using the latest housing-market collapse in 2008 as an example, he points to how the mortgage industry increasingly marketed its products to people who would not have qualified for mortgages under less aggressive market conditions.

While lenders resorted to aggressive – some have called it predatory – lending to susceptible people on the outskirts of credit ratings, those with higher incomes did well investing in all kinds of financial products. However, unlike the credit side of the financial industry, the ability to invest and build wealth was exclusive to those who could do so largely with their own money. As a result, the financial system amplified, even accelerated, existing income differences.

Galbraith's connection between income differences and the different forms of dependency on the financial industry is both fascinating and substantial. An immediate implication is that dependency on the financial system increases in times of slow GDP growth (which is always associated with slow growth in personal income). If we accept the argument made earlier that the welfare state slows down growth, then we can add one factor that contributes to Galbraith's instability mechanism.

By providing cash and in-kind benefits, the welfare state reduces the need for private consumption in certain areas. This liberates income for low-income families that they in turn can use for loan payments. Under a relative poverty concept, the population eligible for entitlement will increase compared to the eligible population under an absolute poverty concept, thus increasing the number of households with more cash on hand for loan payments than their work income otherwise would have merited.

The contribution of the welfare state to Galbraith's financial instability scenario should not be under-estimated, especially in terms of its effects on economic growth. Figure 6.6 reports observations of inflation-adjusted GDP growth and social protection expenditures as a share of GDP for 35 OECD countries:[23]

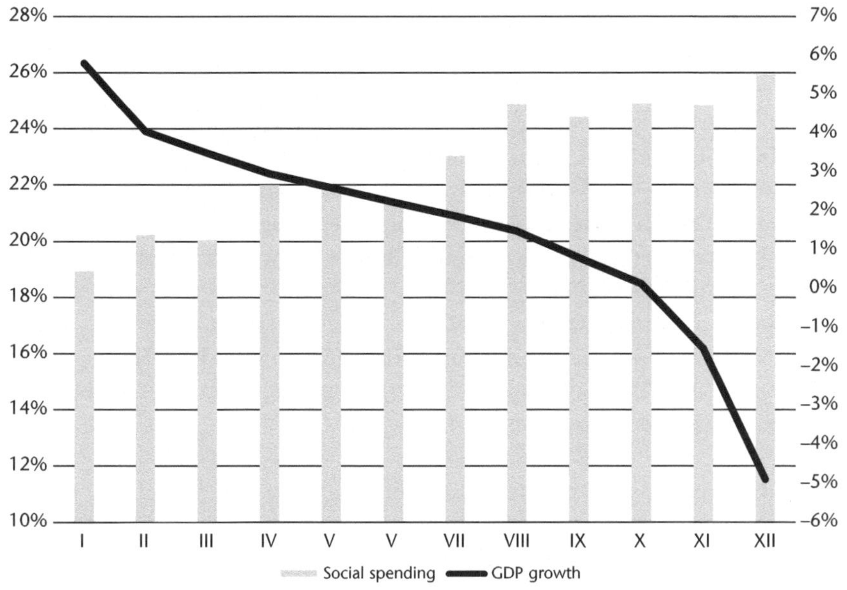

FIGURE 6.6 Social expenditures, share of GDP, real GDP growth

Source: United Nations Statistical Database

Despite convincing evidence to the contrary, advocates of increased social expenditures continue to make their case – and not just from traditional left-of-center sources. Egalitarian arguments favoring increased redistribution spending (which is the real nature of social expenditures) are increasingly popular among voices who, like EITC-advocating Michael Strain of the AEI, one might expect to be more restrictive in support of the welfare state. In recent years, an idea called "basic income guarantee" or "universal basic income" (UBI) has gained supporters deep among the layers of free-market scholars and advocates.

UBI has been a staple of the academic left since at least the 1990s, when it was often marketed as a way to reform entitlement programs for low-income earners. It is almost by definition a program for economic redistribution, as the idea is to pay people for no other reason than they being classified as "eligible."

Recently, UBI has gained new supporters among libertarians. Part of that support is based on the idea that the current welfare system is simply too complicated. In an article from December 2013, Matt Zwolinski at Libertarianism.org referred to research by Cato Institute Senior Fellow Michael Tanner:[24]

> the federal government spent more than $668 billion on over *one hundred and twenty-six* anti-poverty programs in 2012. When you add in the $284 billion spent by state and local governments, that amounts to $20,610 for every poor person in America. Wouldn't it be better just to write the poor a check?

In the erstwhile days of yore, when libertarians advocated the minimal state as defined by Robert Nozick,[25] the obvious response to high per-recipient welfare costs would have been to privatize caring for the poor. Back then, libertarians would argue that the poor would be much better taken care of in the hands of private organizations (such as the Catholic Church, the world's largest charity) than in the arms of the welfare state.

Another voice in the UBI appreciation choir, Libertarian Republic, tries to explain its support with an argument of better efficiency in delivering egalitarian entitlements. The UBI would replace existing programs, including Social Security, Medicare, SNAP and "everything else":[26]

> In their place, we'd receive a streamlined process that would provide new, efficient economic incentives. It is also no small consideration that the federal bureaucracy would substantially recede. All of the complex agencies tasked with administering various programs would become one.

Matt Feeney of the Reason Foundation also endorses UBI.[27] However, unlike Libertarian Republic, his argument is not that one centralized government agency is better than many smaller ones. Instead, his foremost argument is that UBI would treat current recipients of welfare with more dignity:

> Instead of treating those who, often through no fault of their own, have fallen on hard times like children who are incapable of making the right choices about the food they eat or the drugs they may or may not choose to take, why not just give them cash?

This would cut down on administrative costs and, says Feeney, provide incentives for personal responsibility.

Instead of debating principles and their practical applications, on this issue libertarians are in the process of accepting egalitarian principles and limiting the debate to how they should be applied. One such practical question is whether or not there should be any requirements attached to a UBI. Some progressive UBI proponents believe there should be, such as Mathew Forstater, associate professor of economics at the University of Missouri, Kansas City. His version of the UBI is a job-guarantee program where anyone who wants to can go to a local government agency and be given a job for a small but livable wage.[28] You can always get a job and the income, but you have to make the effort of reporting to the job agency.

Notably, the ranks of libertarian UBI supporters would not be complete without a scholar from the American Enterprise Institute. Charles Murray, the AEI's WH Brady Scholar, agrees with Forstater *et al.* on the left: the UBI should come with some strings attached.[29] Murray wants to divide the basic income into three parts: one that is mandated for the purchase of health insurance, one that is designated for retirement savings and one that the recipient can spend as he or she pleases.

Given Murray's eminent reputation as a libertarian political scientist, his endorsement of UBI is more than an endorsement from one scholar. With his support, a voice above the public policy chatter, he points to where the libertarian movement is likely to go in the future. Since the UBI idea is egalitarian in nature, Murray therefore redraws the dividing line between progressive liberalism and libertarianism. The new dividing line puts libertarians on the same side as their left-side peers when it comes to the welfare state. Rather than disposing of a large, redistributive government, UBI-promoting libertarians entrench it, concentrating on operative issues such as: should UBI replace existing welfare programs or add to them? Should there be strings attached, or should everyone get UBI, period?

Even more important than Murray's apparent choice to blur the dividing line between libertarianism and egalitarianism, is that his arguments for forced economic redistribution weakens the case against the welfare state. This is surprising on any day, but all the more serious given the fact that the welfare state is riddled with serious, systemic problems. If egalitarians are not pressured by libertarian or conservative opposition, they may never address the moral problem associated with demoting life from sacrosanctity to an instrument for collective purposes; they may not take seriously the threat that economic stagnation is to the future prosperity of our children; and they may very well continue to ignore the backbreaking burden of national debt continuing to grow in the world's largest welfare states.

To be clear about the egalitarian nature of the UBI, its function as an entitlement program is comparable to that of the EITC, only the UBI would operate on a much larger scale. Nowhere in the libertarian endorsement of UBI is this connection made. On the contrary, Murray's own UBI model actually mimics the EITC down to the minute details, including a built-in marginal tax effect similar to the one in the EITC. In his June 3, 2016 *Wall Street Journal* article, Murray proposes that the UBI should decline as people's incomes increase:

> People can make up to $30,000 in earned income without losing a penny of the [BIG] grant. After $30,000, a graduated surtax reimburses part of the grant, which would drop to $6,500 (but no lower) when an individual reaches $60,000 of earned income. Why should people making good incomes retain any part of the UBI? Because they will be losing Social Security and Medicare, and they need to be compensated.

If libertarians are increasingly going to approve of egalitarian entitlement programs, the chances are dwindling that egalitarians will see the dangers with those programs. Yet so long as the growth-depressing effects of the welfare state remain ignored, the United States will join the rest of the egalitarian world in a slow, but inevitable decline into industrial poverty.

Are America's proponents of the welfare state ready to take seriously the threats of economic stagnation? Are they willing to consider reforms to the welfare state, reforms that would stop our regress into the zero-growth macroeconomic wasteland?

Notes

1 See Larson (2014) for a detailed analysis of these stylized facts, their empirical validity and the consequences for Europe's welfare states.

2 The tax burden is from the same data reported in Figure 6.2 above. GDP growth figures are calculated in national currency, fixed prices, from the UN National Accounts database. The use of two different GDP databases is not recommendable for larger statistical studies, but is tolerable in this small context.

3 Fundamentally, the question of the welfare state and its role in our economy is institutional in nature; ever since econometrics conquered the discipline, economists have shied away from issues that are both complex and practical in nature. More specifically, any economists showing interest in institutional matters are almost certain to become ostracized. Questions about what role institutions play in the economy are usually met with measured derision.

4 This number refers primarily to programs funded by Federal Aid to States. See the Federal Aid to States database provided by the Census Bureau. See also NASBO annual State Expenditure Reports (nasbo.org). Furthermore: Tanner *et al.* (1995), Tanner and Hughes (2013).

5 Persson and Tabellini (1994).

6 Lindbeck *et al.* (1994).

7 Forbes (2000).

8 Arjona *et al.* (2003).

9 Babones (2013).

10 Boushey (2016).

11 Lindbeck (1993).

12 See http://cepr.net/publications/reports/working-moms-and-child-care (accessed May 19, 2017).

13 See www.working-families.org/network/pdf/Effects_PFML_Employment12.pdf (accessed May 19, 2017).

14 See http://nymag.com/daily/intelligencer/2015/02/how-democrats-became-the-child-care-party.html (accessed May 19, 2017).

15 See www.hillaryclinton.com/speeches/remarks-on-working-families-and-her-economic-plan-in-warren-mi/ (accessed May 19, 2017).

16 See http://blogs.wsj.com/washwire/2015/07/13/hillary-clinton-transcript-building-the-growth-and-fairness-economy/ (accessed May 19, 2017).

17 See www.washingtontimes.com/news/2016/jun/7/hillary-clinton-gave-inequality-speech-in-12k-gior/ (accessed May 19, 2017).

18 For a rare example of a repeal plan for the EITC, see: Larson (2012).

19 Strain (2015).

20 See http://kff.org/other/state-indicator/family-coverage/?currentTimeframe=0&sortModel=%7B%22colId%22:%22Location%22,%22sort%22:%22asc%22%7D (accessed May 19, 2017).

21 See www.fns.usda.gov/snap/income-rules-income-limits (accessed May 19, 2017).
22 Galbraith (2012).
23 In the UN database, social expenditures are not reported continuously prior to 2009. Therefore, the observations for the 35 countries are partly in five-year intervals 1980–2005, partly continuous 2009–2014. GDP growth numbers are chosen for the same years. The 35 countries are selected based exclusively on availability of social-expenditure data.
24 See www.libertarianism.org/columns/libertarian-case-basic-income (accessed May 19, 2017).
25 Nozick (1974).
26 See http://thelibertarianrepublic.com/gary-johnson-is-open-to-universal-basic-income/ (accessed May 19, 2017).
27 Feeney (2013).
28 Murray and Forstater (2013).
29 Murray (2016).

7

PROBLEM 3

Government Debt

Related to the question of slow growth is the problem of persistent budget deficits in Europe as well as in the United States. Slow GDP is part of the problem, as it means slow growth in tax revenue. However, the other side of the government budget is as big of a culprit in causing persistent deficits: in a welfare state, government spending is largely defined by entitlement programs, and entitlement spending in turn is determined by variables that are independent of economic growth.

In other words, government spending is driven by legislative decisions that do not take into consideration what the economy can afford. Once entitlement spending has been established based on egalitarian principles, government goes out looking for tax revenue to pay for those programs.

The difference in determinants of tax revenue and government spending creates an inherent discrepancy in the budget of every welfare state. It is therefore not surprising that, over the past 20–30 years, budget deficits have become the norm rather than the exception in the industrialized world.

Slow growth, strong spending: a recipe for chronic deficits

The deficit problem is easily illustrated from both sides of the government budget. To begin with, slow growth and budget deficits correlate with chilling clarity, as clearly illustrated by data from 12 European welfare states from 2002 to 2014. The data, which reports quarterly numbers, shows that GDP growth has to exceed 4 percent per year before these welfare states can hope to balance their budgets, a growth rate unattainable by any welfare state other than as an anomaly (see Figure 7.1).[1]

It is important to keep in mind that slow growth not only erodes tax revenue, but also sends more people into dependency on entitlements for low-income families. Slow growth deprives people of career paths, compensation increases and

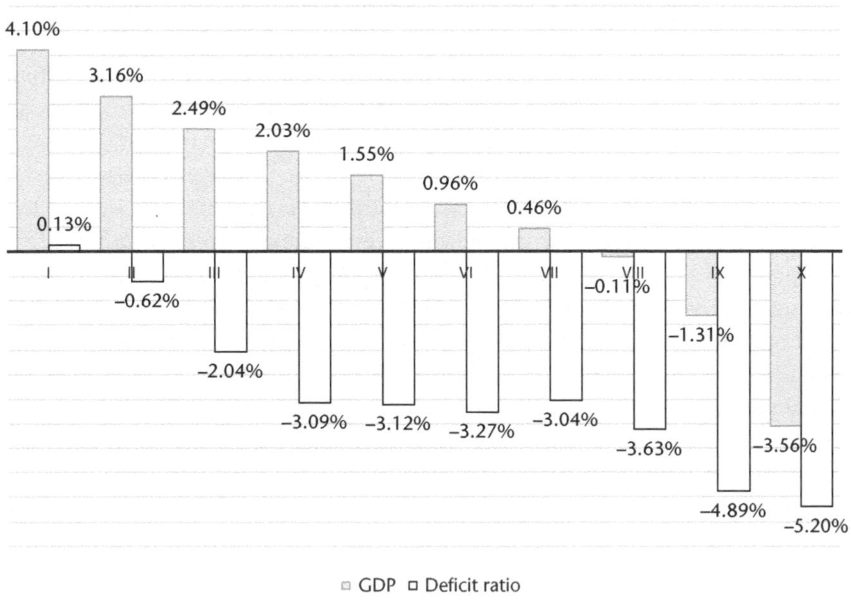

FIGURE 7.1 Budget deficit GDP ratio, real GDP growth: 12 welfare states, 2002–2014

Source: Eurostat

business opportunities. When the economy barely expands, demand for labor is stagnant overall, which easily creates an excess workforce supply. This alone is enough to keep wages stagnant, especially in low-skilled professions where it is easy for new workers to enter. However, the more persistent the growth problem becomes, the more widespread the excess-supply problem becomes in the labor market: low-skilled workers who cannot get ahead in their line of work pursue professional and academic education, hoping for work in higher-skilled segments of the labor market. As the economic stagnation drags out in time, segment after segment is filled up with hopeful, newly educated professionals pursuing a stagnant number of jobs.

As excess supply of labor becomes a permanent phenomenon, the entire workforce experiences a stagnation of compensation. More and more of them qualify for more and more benefits under the welfare state, pushing up demand for government spending – while the same stagnation in workforce compensation puts a lid on tax revenues.

In most welfare states, the problem of chronic budget deficits did not become pervasive until the 1990s. It was foreseen by early welfare-state proponents such as Gunnar Myrdal and John Kenneth Galbraith, whose proposals for strong growth and various forms of economic planning were intended to prevent deficits in the first place. Yet when the slowdown in GDP growth began taking permanent proportions during the 1980s, egalitarian politicians in, primarily, Europe did not heed the warning signals. As a result, the welfare states persisted as complex systems of entitlement spending, thus inevitably leading first Europe, then the United States, into the dangerous macroeconomic territory where budget deficits and economic stagnation are inextricably tied together.

Yet any attempt to break out of this state of industrial poverty is hampered by the fact that government, with its roster of entitlement programs, has made a long list of promises to its citizenry that it will have a difficult time getting out of. An entitlement program is promise of a service, provided by government, where spending is driven by what government has promised, to whom and for what period of time. (It is no exaggeration to say that tax revenue is the last variable to affect government spending.) If government promises child care to all families with small children, then in order for that promise to be meaningful – so parents can rely on it for planning their lives – government must maintain that promise in its entirety, for the foreseeable future.

For example, a child-care promise will have to cap the number of children per teacher and set a minimum standard for the facilities and conditions under which children will be taken care of.

Right here, a budget for the entitlement has been established, a budget that is determined with no regard to what taxpayers can or cannot afford.

Even if the standards of child-care facilities are determined with reference to an estimate of taxes that are affordable when the program is created, child-care spending over time will be driven by the cost of the products necessary to maintain the government promise – not by what the tax base can pay for.

In practice, minor adjustments to entitlement programs take place on a regular basis. Many of them are directly related to the funding situation: a school district waits to hire a new teacher until the next budget year begins, making children put up with substitutes; patients relying on Medicare for their pharmaceutical drugs may find, on occasion, that there are unexpected changes in the supply of drugs covered by their Medicare plan.

However, in order to maintain its entitlement promises, government must keep intact the defining features of its entitlement programs. Sooner or later, the cost of entitlement programs runs away from its tax base.

At this point, an argument is often put forward in defense of the welfare state, suggesting that when government provides for some of our needs, we can focus more of our time on work and more of our money on private consumption. For example, when a family does not have to pay out of pocket for child care; when they do not have to spend their own parental time caring for their children during daytime; they can increase their workforce participation. They also adjust their consumption as they have now been relieved of a major, regular expense. Assuming that the need to provide child care prior to the government program restricted their workforce participation and consumption, the average family benefiting from a child-care entitlement and increases its labor supply and its monthly expenses. Both of these have positive effects on the economy.

A similar argument could be made in favor of a single-payer health-care system as well as of a tax-funded paid family leave program.

At the same time, all entitlement programs have a dampening effect on growth, starting with the egalitarian funding model that is almost universally applied in the world's welfare states. An entitlement program is egalitarian by definition, which – in addition to the conditions of qualifying for the program – means that the average beneficiary cannot be the average provider of funds for the program. Egalitarianism in practice necessitates that the family benefiting from government child care has a comparatively low income, and that the family providing funds for the program is comparatively well paid.

With egalitarian principles guiding the taxation side of the equation, the burden of funding entitlements falls disproportionately on higher-income families. Higher taxes discourage the economic activity on which the taxes are levied. Individual families may respond differently to the tax that pays for government child care; in the aggregate, the reaction will be negative in the form of reduced workforce participation, reduced entrepreneurship and – as disposable income declines – a drop in private consumption.

As a basic rule, all entitlement programs have a negative effect on economic activity by means of their funding, but only some entitlement programs have a positive effect through their spending. The negative effects are, relatively speaking, less drastic in a welfare state where in-kind services dominate the roster of entitlements; the American welfare state, which emphasizes in-kind benefits,[2] appears to have been less vulnerable to a growth slowdown than its European peers. This could explain, in part, why it has taken a bit longer for the U.S. economy to be harmed by low growth; nevertheless, its entitlement programs are not designed to spend money in tune with the tax base that provides for them.

Looking strictly at the federal government, there is no doubt that entitlement promises outpace the tax base (approximately 80 percent of federal tax revenue comes from personal income) and that they do so on a permanent, structural basis. Since 1960, federal entitlement spending has grown by 9.3 percent per year. During that same period, personal income has grown by only 6.8 percent per year on average. For every $100 in new entitlement spending that Congress has allowed, personal income has only grown by $73.

Figure 7.2 displays the structural over-promising built into federal entitlement spending. Suppose we started in 1960 with $100 in entitlement spending and $100 in personal income tax revenue. By 1970 entitlement spending is at $263.69, while personal income has only grown to $214.43.

In 1980 entitlement spending is 84 percent larger than personal income; in 2015 it is 123 percent larger.

Faced with this long-term funding gap, the United States government has had three options: reform away the egalitarian nature of its spending programs; raise taxes; or use deficit as a permanent form of funding.

It has chosen the third option, which exposes the federal government – and the entire U.S. economy – to serious macroeconomic risks associated with large debt.

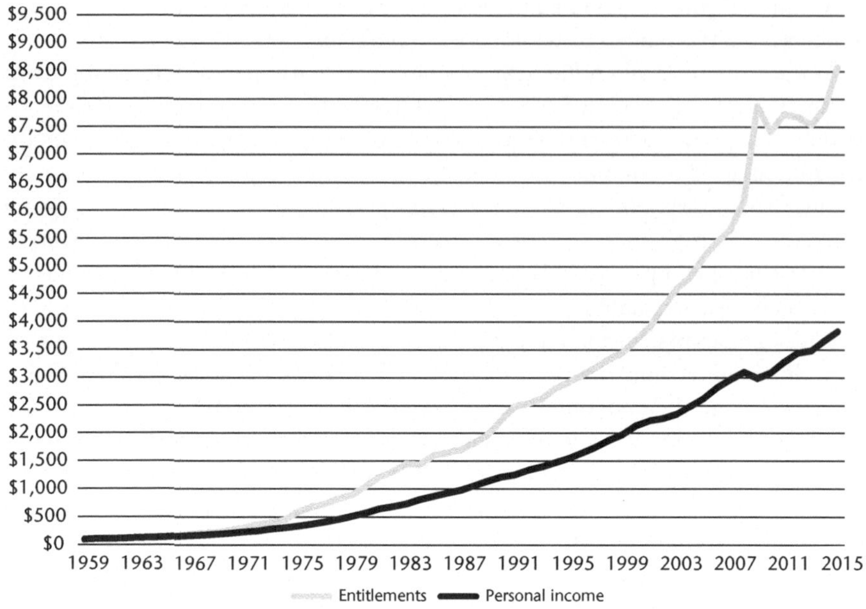

FIGURE 7.2 Growth rates, current prices: federal entitlement spending and personal income

Source: Bureau of Economic Analysis; Office of Management and Budget

Austerity and the Great Recession

Persistent deficits and slow growth push welfare states to a point of fiscal panic, in other words a situation where financial markets lose faith in a nation's government debt, and said government has no choice but to take immediate, short-sighted and sizable action to reduce its deficits. The policies taken under such circumstances are sometimes referred to as austerity. The term has a broader use, often referring generally to reductions in government spending, however it has been popularized by episodes of fiscal panic in, primarily, European welfare states over the past 30 years.

The Great Recession, which started in late 2008, made austerity a household term by hurling many of Europe's welfare states into fiscal panic. Over several years prior to the crisis, persistent deficits had built up unsustainable levels of government debt. In a very short time, deeply indebted countries saw their ability to fund deficits collapse into a race against a clock, set by international financial investors.

It has become conventional wisdom that the Great Recession was a financial crisis, and therefore had nothing to do with the debt levels in individual countries. That is incorrect: the crisis was primarily not a financial crisis, but a crisis of unsustainable government borrowing. As explained above, borrowing becomes a permanent funding arm for welfare states when GDP growth slows down permanently. For this reason, the Great Recession is the most significant macroeconomic episode in the history of the welfare state: it puts an end to endless expansion of government under seeming impunity from the structural problems built into a government with large entitlement programs.

Already in the early days of the Great Recession, starting in 2009, there were signs that this was not a financial crisis. International credit rating agencies issued numerous warnings that welfare states with deficit problems were jeopardizing their credit. The list of treasury bonds that were no longer minimum-risk investments grew rapidly during the opening act of the Great Recession.

As for the financial industry, it did indeed go through a crisis, but it did not originate within the financial industry. As the economic crisis unfolded, financial institutions experienced dwindling non-financial business loan demand. Their outstanding loans were subject to higher default risk, which is perfectly normal when the economy enters a recession. This created a climate where, in order to issue new loans, banks would be particularly cautious about credit risk.

This is where the losses suffered by financial institutions tie over to the welfare-state debt crisis. Normally, treasury bonds would be a good investment to counter increased risk in the non-financial credit market. Therefore, it would be logical for financial institutions, at the beginning of the Great Recession, to expand investment in those bonds by financial institutions.

However, there was nothing normal about Europe's treasury-bond market. Contrary to what theory would prescribe, and history suggest, it was drifting into higher-risk waters. At that point, financial institutions taking credit losses would be perfectly right in shying away from government debt.

They did not. For reasons that have been given insufficient attention in the literature, they expanded their investments in troubled treasury bonds.

The reasons for this are directly related to the attempts by governments in European welfare states to preserve their egalitarian projects; to save their entitlement programs from an emerging free-market verdict over excessive spending in an era of inadequate economic growth.

In 2009–2013, four years when Europe's economies were performing worse than they ever had since World War II, financial institutions increased their ownership of downgraded government debt by 55 percent. Some examples:

- *Ireland.* In April 2009 Moody's put the Irish government on downgrade watch, executing the first of a total of five downgrades three months later.
- That same year the Irish government added €24.6 billion to its debt, and financial institutions bought 78 percent of that new debt.
- In 2010, when Fitch added two Irish downgrades to those by Moody's,[3] the Dublin government borrowed €39.5 billion. Financial institutions purchased 59 percent of it.

- In 2011 Standard & Poor's added to Moody's downgrades while Fitch put Ireland on yet another downgrade watch.[4]
- At this point, though, financial institutions hesitated: after having bought two thirds of the downgraded nation's new debt in the past two years, they actually reduced their holdings of Irish debt by €4.5 billion.

Some of that reduction was reversed in 2012, but overall they stabilized their exposure to Irish treasury bonds.

- *Spain.* In June 2010 Moody's put Spain on downgrade watch.
- In the following two years they downgraded the Spanish government's credit rating five times.
- During that time the Spanish government borrowed €323 billion, of which financial institutions picked up 71 percent.
- This amount, €230 billion, was more than three times as much as financial institutions had invested in Spanish debt over the seven years preceding the Great Recession.

This massive new investment happened while the Spanish government's credit rating was tumbling.

- *Portugal* went on Moody's downgrade watch in May 2010, followed by a downgrade in July that year.
- Another four downgrades took place in the following 18 months.
- Despite its declining credit rating, in 2010–2012 the government in Lisbon was able to borrow another €64 billion.
- Financial institutions bought 55 percent of the new debt.

- *Italy* was put on downgrade watch in June 2011.
- In the following 12 months the country was hit by three downgrades.
- The response from financial institutions was almost absurd: in 2011 they purchased 67 percent of the Italian government's newly issued debt.
- However, in 2012 they bought more than twice what the government needed to borrow for that year!

For the entire two years when Italy's credit went into tailspin, financial institutions purchased €203.5 billion worth of Italian government debt – €66 billion *more* than what the government needed to borrow.

- *France* lost its AAA rating with Standard & Poor's in January 2012.[5]
- In November that year Moody's downgraded France,[6] followed by Fitch in July of 2013[7] and yet another downgrade by S&P in November 2013.[8]
- Since no downgrade comes without prior warning signs, it is notable that during 2010–2012 the French government borrowed €341 billion, of which

financial institutions bought 44 percent, or €150 billion.

- But not only that: the financial-institution share of the debt purchases actually accelerated as France came closer to a downgrade, as they bought:
  - 16.3 percent of new French debt in 2010;
  - 45.6 percent in 2011; and
  - 66.5 percent in 2012.

The 2012 purchases are remarkable given that Standard & Poor's January 2012 French downgrade came with big fanfare:[9]

> Standard & Poor's swept the debt-ridden European continent with punishing credit downgrades Friday, stripping France of its coveted AAA status and dropping Italy even lower. Germany retained its top-notch rating, but Portugal's debt was consigned to junk. In all, S&P lowered the ratings of nine countries.

In four of the five most troubled welfare states in Europe, financial institutions bought massive amounts of treasury bonds right as the crisis escalated. (Eurostat does not report this kind of data for Greece, the most troubled of Europe's welfare states.) From 2010 to 2012 their purchases of bonds from these four countries topped €392 billion. For comparison, in 2010–2012 the total amount that financial institutions invested in treasury bonds from the entire group of countries (the 21 that publish this kind of data) was €633 billion.

Consider this for a moment. Financial institutions, cautiously navigating an economy in a steep downturn, can choose to buy treasury bonds from 21 different countries. They allocate 62 percent of their treasury-bond purchases to four of those countries with notably bad credit.

How were all these investments made possible? What could motivate financial institutions, under pressure from an escalating recession, to further escalate the risk profile of their portfolios?

As soon as governments in Europe's most troubled welfare states saw their credit ratings drop, they resorted to fiscal-panic driven austerity. Governments focused their fiscal policies on raising taxes and cutting government spending; generally, the harder they were pressured by financial investors, the tougher their austerity measures got. Their main concern was to please investors in the treasury-bond market, win their confidence back and thereby find a way back to normal fiscal circumstances.

A major problem with austerity policies is that it suppresses economic activity. Completely in compliance with traditional Keynesian macroeconomics, countries with the toughest austerity policies have suffered the most in terms of growth suppression. Figure 7.3 reports the trade-off forced upon welfare states under austerity. It contrasts quarterly data for government debt as share of GDP against real GDP growth, aggregated for the entire euro zone (configured as it is today). The debt ratio (dark gray line; left axis) is shown to increase almost uninterruptedly from 1997 to early 2010. This increase in the debt ratio is the result of slow GDP growth (light gray line; right axis) and increases in government spending that are not capped to the annual growth in inflation-adjusted GDP.

It is particularly notable that the debt ratio grows when GDP growth is rising, as it did in 1997–2000 and 2003–2008:

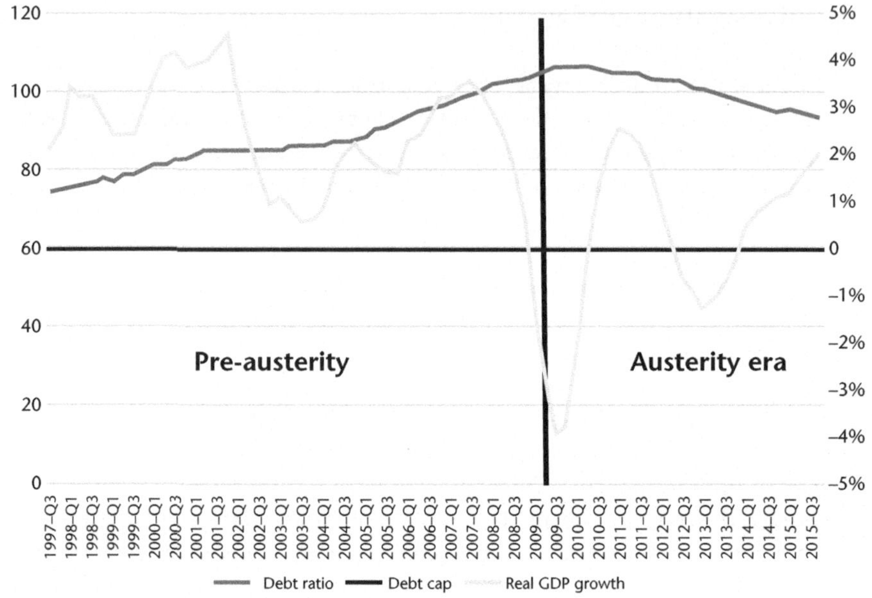

FIGURE 7.3 Euro zone actual debt, debt limit, real GDP growth

Source: Eurostat

A rising debt when the economy is growing and operating at or close to full employment is akin to a structural budget deficit, that is, a deficit that outlasts the business cycle. A structural deficit, in turn, is caused by a permanent imbalance between government spending and revenue. This imbalance has its root cause in the nature of government spending: an entitlement program is a spending promise to a designated group of entitled individuals which is made independently of the ability of taxpayers to pay for it.

Government-provided health care is a good example. Regardless of whether the promise is universal – covering the entire population – or selective as with Medicaid, the group of people defined as entitled have now been promised a set of medical services without having to pay individually for those services. This means that:

1 The entitlement is defined in kind, meaning the total cost of the program is a function of the nature of the services promised, not the other way around.
2 If the provision of medical services under the entitlement program increases, then the cost of the program automatically rises, regardless of whether taxpayers can afford it or not.
3 Entitled citizens adjust their private finances to the government promise, expecting the package of services to largely stay the same over time.

The first point is an open-ended promise in terms of the money that government will have to commit to its entitlement program. The second point means that there is a built-in cost-increase factor in the entitlement program, raising the cost of the promised services regardless of whether the economy is in a recession or a growth period. Together, these two points make budget deficits inevitable during recessions.

If a large enough number of entitlement programs are added together, with the same structure in place as defined by the first two points above, then the sum total of all government spending promises easily add up to a structural deficit. The structural budget imbalance is neither automatic nor necessary, but it can easily be the cumulative result of a long period of welfare-state expansion. As Figure 7.3 above indicates, this is precisely what happened in Europe in general.

A structural deficit leads to a build-up of government debt which, sooner or later, leads to the questioning of the government's credit worthiness. The Great Recession, regardless of its cause, laid bare the over-indebtedness of a number of welfare states in Europe. As the growth in tax revenue stagnated or declined, the gap between debt payment obligations and debt funding raised enough concerns among lenders to cause a debt crisis.

One of the key experiences from the Great Recession is that governments are limited in their ability to use deficits as a regular funding mechanism for their spending promises. This experience is not limited to Europe's welfare states, but applies everywhere a government has built a system of entitlements with spending promises that are not capped by taxpayers' ability to pay for them.

The United States is no exception to this mechanism. The major difference between the U.S. welfare state and its European peers is in the pace at which it has expanded. Where Scandinavian and some continental European welfare states have grown rapidly, the American welfare state has moved forward at a snail's pace by comparison. This has also slowed down the progress by which the United States approaches the point where creditors consider its debt to be unsustainable. That point, however, will come.

As the United States so clearly demonstrates, a legislature is not fiscally restricted in its pursuit of egalitarianism by its taxpayers' ability to fund that pursuit. The ultimate restriction is instead the debt cap imposed by global creditors. However, when a nation reaches that restriction, the awakening can be rude indeed. Europe's austerity experience during the Great Recession is a serious reminder of what that restriction can do to a welfare state.

Because of the easiness with which legislators in both Europe and the United States have been able to make deficits a regular source of budget funding, austerity is a practically unavoidable consequence of the welfare state. In *Industrial Poverty*, published in 2014, right on the heels of the Great Recession, Larson gives a detailed account of austerity policies in Denmark (Chapter 5), Sweden (Chapter 2), Greece, Spain, Italy (Chapter 4a), France, Cyprus, Portugal, the Netherlands and the Czech Republic (Chapter 4b). The Danish and Swedish experiences date back to the 1980s and 1990s, respectively, but the others are concentrated in the Great Recession.

The actual execution of austerity differs from one country to the next, in terms of both content and intensity. The content is always a combination of revenue-increasing measures (primarily tax increases, secondarily increases in fees for government services) and spending reductions, but some countries put more emphasis on one over the other.

Intensity is the size of the fiscal measures per period of time; the Swedish austerity program from the 1990s remains the most intense to date, where combinations of tax increases and spending reductions amounted to almost 3 percent of GDP per year for a period of three years. By comparison, if imposed on the $18-trillion U.S. GDP, a 3 percent austerity program would have raised taxes and cut spending by a total of $540 billion per year, for three years.

While the immediate purpose of austerity is to eliminate a budget deficit and thereby calm the financial waters where the welfare-state ship is sailing, the implied purpose is to adjust the size of the welfare state to what its tax base can be expected to afford. That purpose, however, is rarely if ever brought up in the context of austerity. There is scant evidence of such considerations in the political or public-policy discussions in austerity-ridden countries; the unpleasant experiences with harsh fiscal measures have not led to a questioning of the fundamental reasons as to why welfare states end up under such pressure that austerity is the only way out.

Austerity, credit rating and financial institutions

It is not difficult to see how governments under fiscal-panic pressure would try to avoid harsh austerity measures. Not only do such policies cause political resistance, even turmoil (as in Greece), but they are also disruptive from a macroeconomic viewpoint. Tax increases in already high-taxed economies accelerate an economic downturn, while cuts to government spending disrupt private sector economic activity. For example, cuts in health care force people to wait longer for treatment, holding them back from working; cuts in income-security programs reduce people's disposable income.

There is also an ideological aspect of austerity that raises the bar for governments under pressure to reduce their deficits. Egalitarianism is a major, long-term commitment, forming a welfare state that takes decades to build and monumental political effort to execute. Once it is up and running, large segments of the population depend on its entitlements for their daily livelihood. It is not easy for leading politicians in a country under fiscal-panic stress to give up the welfare state and simply start rolling back its entitlement programs.

When the credit rating of a welfare state declines, its government is left with very few options in order to continue spending on its welfare programs. The room for tax increases is limited if it exists at all, and running more deficits – the alternative, quasi-permanent funding option – is the very reason that financial markets are losing confidence in the country's treasury bonds in the first place.

The only option left is for the central bank to print money. By adding new money supply, the central bank can buy bonds directly from the treasury. The problem for Europe's welfare states, as they fell into the debt dungeon in the early days of the Great Recession, is that they were part of the euro zone. Under the charter that defined the European Central Bank (ECB) as well as the EU constitution, the ECB is not allowed to either lend to indebted governments (by buying bonds from the treasury) or buy treasury bonds on the open market.

Such bans, however, did not prevent the ECB from intervening on behalf of the credit-troubled welfare states under its monetary jurisdiction. Contrary to the very intentions behind the construction of Europe's common currency and its central bank, from 2008 to 2012 the ECB massively expanded its lending to governments. As reported in the ECB's January 2017 MFI Balance Sheets online report, the ECB expanded lending to governments by 8–15 percent per year almost every year during the Great Recession (and continued to do so again after a brief pause in 2014).[10]

Even more conspicuous is the ECB's use of its program to rescue troubled banks as a tool for funding welfare states with major credit problems. In a 2012 interview, renowned economist Willem Buiter, an established authority on the European economy, predicted that EU member-state governments as well as the European Central Bank would "continue" to pressure banks to buy treasury bonds.[11] Furthermore, in an article on March 10, 2014, on the risks associated with banks holding large amounts of government debt, Reuters reported that the ECB has been criticized for having poured gasoline on the proverbial fire. When banks got cheap loans, at a cost of 0.25–1 percent, they were able to make easy profits by investing those loans in government securities with a yield of 7 percent or more:[12]

> Cash-strapped peripheral banks – many of which have been shut out of primary markets – have welcomed the opportunity to plug capital shortfalls, ploughing over half of their net borrowings from the ECB's emergency longer-term refinancing operations facility into bonds, while lending a mere 13 percent to the real economy, according to JP Morgan figures.

In other words, it was central-bank policy to eliminate market pricing of treasury-bond risk. As a direct consequence, and consistent with Austrian economic theory, this policy change led financial institutions to do exactly that: stop relying on market pricing of risk. They shifted their own risk policy from risk aversion to risk neutrality, explaining their massive investments in otherwise risky government debt during the Great Recession.

A lesson for America's egalitarians

The ECB policies to support troubled welfare states with newly minted cash is destructive over the long term. It floods the economy with excess liquidity at a time when there are limited investment opportunities in a stagnant economy. Since financial institutions eventually come to sit on the excess liquidity, they become prone to lending it for speculative purposes. Alas, the stock market performs remarkably well in an economy with excessive liquidity.

In addition to the threat of speculative bubbles on equity markets, a rapid increase in money supply for the purposes of purchasing treasury bonds blows new life into an unsustainable welfare-state funding model. Government spending continues at a disproportionately high level while there are no changes in the macroeconomic conditions of the private sector. There is no change to the structural imbalance between spending and tax revenue; it is important to remember that this structural imbalance was the cause of the excess printing of money in the first place. When, over the long term, government spending outgrows the tax base, deficit funding becomes virtually permanent as entitlement funding; eventually, the annual increase in government debt is met with costly credit downgrades – and the central bank steps in to save the day.

Over an extended period of time, continuous excess expansion of the money supply jeopardizes price stability. It is important to note that monetary inflation is a rare phenomenon that occurs only under special circumstances, but as Venezuela and, to a lesser degree, Argentina have demonstrated in recent years, no economy is immune to monetary hyper-inflation. If government insists on perpetuating a fiscally unsustainable welfare state, then eventually its egalitarian stubbornness will even bring about uncontrollable price increases.

The big question from an American viewpoint is to what extent the European experience can be put to good use. The United States has been borrowing money for its entitlement spending longer and more consistently than any other welfare state, yet its debt problem has only recently resulted in tangible punishments by credit rating institutes. Furthermore, when the U.S. government was downgraded in 2011, it did not have the same drastic effect on the U.S. economy as the downgrades of European countries had. One reason for this is the reliance of the U.S. Treasury on the Federal Reserve's Quantitative Easing programs, which partly shielded it from market forces. Another reason is the unique international status of the U.S. dollar, which has helped Congress in its insistence on continuous use of deficits to fund part of federal spending.

In a few short words: can the American welfare state continue to exist as it is without pulling the country into a fiscal-panic situation similar to what European welfare states have experienced?

The even shorter answer to this question is: no. The country suffers from the same growth problems as the European economy; the Trump presidency has added a somewhat brighter outlook on growth in the next few years, but unless the Trump administration and Congress make structural changes to the welfare state's growth-discouraging tax and entitlement systems, those brighter forecasts will turn out to be nothing more than that.

Furthermore, judging from the election of Donald Trump as the 45th president, and the ability of the Republicans to maintain control over both Congressional chambers, it is fair to say that a substantial part of the American people would not welcome higher taxes. Resistance to higher taxes under the Obama administration, as well as the popularity of tax cuts under Presidents Reagan and Bush, indicate that Americans in general are unwilling to surrender more of their earnings to government. There is also a tendency among Americans to move from high-tax states to low-tax states, adding to their expression of aversion to high taxes.[13]

With the tax-hike avenue to fund the American welfare state closed, only two options remain: continuous borrowing or spending cuts. The latter option has never been consistently put to work, while the former has become so permanent it rarely gets any attention in the public-policy debate. Yet the worry about the long-term consequences of the national debt is real, even in Congress whose members have introduced more than a dozen bills over the past 35 years to put a balanced-budget amendment on the U.S. Constitution. They have also passed a number of other bills aimed at making deficit spending more difficult.

Interest groups and individual public-finance scholars have contributed to the discussion with their own balanced-budget proposals. However, to some researchers, the fact that Congress, despite all these attempts, has been able to continue its seemingly endless streak of annual deficits is an indication that focus should be on other options, primarily spending cuts.

This is where the American debate over austerity differentiates itself from the conversation over the same term in Europe. Unlike Americans, many Europeans have had first-hand experience of the kind of spending cuts – and tax increases – that come with austerity policies. In fact, the European experience continues to say this: at present, early 2017, the Greek austerity tragedy is still unfolding. Many other European countries are still struggling with the aftermath of their own austerity experiences.

Since austerity has not yet hit the United States, it is understandable that the debate remains somewhat distanced from its actual European consequences. Nevertheless, it is crucial that America's egalitarians, in their desire to preserve the welfare state, pay close attention to the austerity issue. Since Congress is very unlikely to raise taxes, and since the Federal Reserve under Janet Yellen has shown at least some interest in permanently ending its Quantitative Easing commitments, the roster of fiscal-policy options available to Congress is rather thin.

Spending cuts essentially remain as the only viable option. The question is whether Congress will execute structured cuts, or hold out until pushed into the fiscal-panic corner by further credit downgrades and financial markets losing faith in the U.S. Treasury.

In an attempt to influence their choice, American policy experts continue to debate austerity. Assuming for a moment that the term is unaffiliated with fiscal crises, thus meaning "spending cuts" in general, there is a case to be made for it based on the European experience. The effect of austerity on welfare-state spending is, namely, visible in Eurostat data over social-protection outlays within the European Union. In 2004–2009, social-protection spending in the euro zone increased by 4.4 percent per year. By contrast, in 2010–2012 the annual increase was only 2.2 percent. This is despite the fact that rapidly rising unemployment increased demand for social-protection programs: from 2008 to 2010 a total of 4 million Europeans lost their jobs; another 2 million were added to the unemployment lines through 2012.

As Table 7.1 shows, austerity was even more visible in some countries:

TABLE 7.1 Effects of austerity changes in social-protection spending

	2004–2009	*2010–2012*
Lithuania	17.02%	–1.89%
Latvia	15.39%	–0.17%
Spain	8.89%	0.36%
Poland	8.35%	2.54%
Greece	8.32%	–2.86%
Hungary	5.63%	–0.04%
Portugal	5.62%	–0.73%
Italy	4.49%	1.64%

The problem is that none of these countries has fundamentally changed its government-spending structures. In no case has the welfare state been phased out or even substantially reduced. Austerity has not served the purpose of structurally altering the role of government in the economy – in other words it has not challenged the egalitarian project – but instead aimed to make it more affordable, a better fit for a smaller tax base.

Down the road, this means that the same problems that led to this round of austerity will arise once again. Britain is a good example, having been through several episodes of austerity in the past. One of those episodes, in 1992, led to the collapse of sterling under international speculative pressure.

Based on its experience from the early 1990s, Britain was politically relatively well prepared when the Great Recession hit in 2009. It were more able to handle a rapid deficit increase than most other European countries. Rather than taking to panic-driven austerity measures, the British government simply chose to allow a measured increase in the budget deficit and instead put more money into welfare-state spending. While the budget deficit averaged 8.5 percent of GDP in 2010–2012, welfare-state spending increased by 7.8 percent per year.

With this strategy, the government in London was able to avoid the financial, fiscal, political and macroeconomic turmoil that comes with harsh austerity measures. At the same time, the very fact that it had to accept another rise in deficits – and thereby yet another pile-up of debt for future generations to pay for – is face evidence that austerity, as practiced in Europe, is not a permanent solution to the welfare state's deficit-funding problem.

Switzerland has tried another path forward. Having debt-capping measures worked into their laws, the Swiss avoided serious austerity episodes during the Great Recession. The country has some limits on welfare-state spending that are absent in most other European countries: they do not have a single-payer health insurance system, and their fiscal policy is comparatively decentralized along the principles of a federation. Generally, though, the Swiss government has avoided excessive entitlement spending under a fiscal-policy feature colloquially known as the "Swiss debt brake." Dan Mitchell, economist and senior fellow with the Cato Institute, explains:[14]

> Before the law went into effect in 2003, government spending was expanding by an average of 4.3 percent per year. Since then it's increased by only 2.6 percent annually. The Swiss debt brake does not require a balanced budget in the traditional sense. Tax receipts, as we know from the American experience, tend to increase rapidly when the economy is doing well and fall off when the economy stumbles. To smooth out the ups and downs, Switzerland's debt brake limits spending growth to average revenue increases over a multiyear period (as calculated by the Swiss Federal Department of Finance).

This mechanism has been relatively successful, as Mitchell has pointed out in follow-up articles in his blog.[15] New evidence reinforces Mitchell's conclusions, suggesting the measure may be an option for the U.S. government to consider.[16] It would likely help Congress avoid being overwhelmed by fiscal panic, but it is an open question whether or not it would eventually protect the U.S. economy from fiscal-panic episodes. The Swiss experience is too thin to provide a definitive answer.

The structural problem with the welfare state remains even under a Swiss-style debt management system. Entitlement programs will continue to grow according to their built-in growth parameters: the number of eligible people, the quantity and quality of the service they are promised, the inflation built into the cost of that service, and the duration of their eligibility.

This structural problem will remain so long as the welfare state remains. Unfortunately, one must once again note that very little – if any – attention is given to the welfare state and its fundamental role in causing the government debt problem. In fact, when it comes to the debate over the U.S. debt problem, it is easy to get the impression that those who should be the welfare state's biggest critics – whose contributions could help keep egalitarians on their toes – have effectively conceded defeat. Instead of developing intelligent alternatives to the welfare state's system of entitlements, some of them resort to proposing austerity as a means to keep government spending in check, or affect some reductions in it.

A good example is Veronique de Rugy, senior research fellow with the Mercatus Center at George Mason University. She is of the opinion that if austerity consists exclusively of spending cuts, it will be an instrument for reducing the size of government.[17] Such a reduction, de Rugy implies, would be the beginning of a process that would bring about limited government.

As Larson explains (2014, pp. 173–179), de Rugy is mistaken. Austerity relying exclusively on spending cuts can help a government reach budget balance faster, with less harm inflicted on growth, so long as the purpose is just that: to combine stronger growth with a balanced budget. If, on the other hand, the purpose is to permanently reduce the size of government, the spending cuts employed under austerity will not achieve that goal. They will constitute a temporary reduction of entitlement spending, with no match in tax cuts, leaving recipients of cash and in-kind benefits worse off.

That is, until austerity ends. At that point, all entitlement programs still exist, as do the criteria that determine people's eligibility. Once austerity is ended, those criteria will guarantee a return to growth in government spending. Since government spending will once again grow independently of the tax base – the standard setting for the welfare state – the deficit that austerity cured will flare up again, no later than in the next recession.

This particular aspect of austerity-driven spending cuts is left unattended to by the free-market-oriented literature. The reason for this omission – a glaring one given its significance in separating austerity success from austerity failure – is a mystery.

One possible explanation is that free-market scholars over time have decided to accept the fact that the welfare state exists, and will continue to do so for the foreseeable future. Instead of developing reforms that permanently reduce the size of entitlement programs, or eliminate them altogether, the free-market-based public-policy literature is increasingly concentrated on devising strategies for making the welfare state more affordable to taxpayers.

There is a long line of libertarian and conservative scholars behind de Rugy. Waiting to contribute to a job only Sisyphus could enjoy, in 2014 a group of free-market scholars representing the cream of the crust of America's right-of-center think tanks set out to make the American welfare state fiscally sustainable. Working jointly with academic and foreign peers, representatives of the Heritage Foundation, the Cato Institute and the Mercatus Center penned a report that essentially admitted that Gunnar Myrdal and John Kenneth Galbraith were correct – both analytically and morally.[18]

The story of their report, titled *Europe's Fiscal Crisis Revealed*, begins with the usual pledge of allegiance to limited government and a declaration that austerity somehow is an instrument for getting there. However, the report quickly moves on to explain that austerity really is all about reducing budget deficits. In the preface, Derrick Morgan, Vice President for Economic Freedom and Opportunity at the Heritage Foundation, defends both the term and the practice of austerity:

> This report demonstrates that not all methods of fiscal restraint were equal: Increasing taxes was more damaging to the economy and less effective in reducing deficits than spending cuts. The effective way to shrink deficits – reducing spending – leads to stronger economic growth over time, while the counterproductive way – tax increases – leads to slower economic growth and lingering ill effects with less deficit reduction than advertised.

Alas, Morgan admits that austerity cannot be about reducing the size of government if it is also a fiscal strategy to balance the government budget. Morgan and his co-authors acknowledge that a balanced government budget serves the latter purpose, namely making the welfare state fiscally sustainable.

In fairness, they also express hope that a balanced budget will lead to stronger growth – which in turn will contribute to the welfare state's fiscal sustainability. However, compared to the overwhelming success of the egalitarian project ever since the beginning of the War on Poverty, the ambition to strengthen funding for the welfare state barely rises above eclectic flea killing. Effectively, Morgan and his co-authors only go as far as to admitting – without reference – that they have learned the lesson about economic growth from the arch egalitarians Gunnar and Alva Myrdal and John Kenneth Galbraith.

Of course, the group of supposed free-market writers do not make any references to their intellectual predecessors, but that does not stop them from effectively declaring that the egalitarians have won. The welfare state is here to say and all that matters is to find a way to solve its persistent deficit problem.

As if to set the stage for this massive concession of defeat from America's leading libertarians and conservatives, Alberto Alesina, lead researcher for *Europe's Fiscal Crisis Revealed*, flagged it up a year earlier. In an article for *Forbes Magazine*, co-authored with Veronique de Rugy, Alesina stated that not all austerity is the same:[19]

> There is "austerity" and there is austerity. "Austerity" implemented through tax hikes is harmful, but austerity based on appropriate spending cuts is the best way to reduce a country's public debt burden. Implementing pro-growth reforms as part of the fiscal adjustment process can minimize any economic cost that budget cuts may have.

In a conference paper a year later, Alesina and a group of other economists again defined austerity as a means toward fiscal consolidation, that is, reductions in budget deficits and nothing else.[20] Its purpose was again to fiscally secure the egalitarian project for the foreseeable future.

The welfare state on supply-side life support

An effort by leading libertarian and conservative scholars to try to save the welfare state is likely to center in on supply-side economics. It has been tried under Presidents Reagan and Bush, and it is likely going to be tried again under President Trump.

There are reasons why Trump's advisors would commit to a third round of growth-oriented tax cuts. During the Reagan presidency the U.S. economy experienced one of its most remarkable turnarounds ever: from the high-inflation, high-unemployment stagflation years of the late 1970s, Reagan's tax cuts, inspired by supply-side theory, helped bring about one of the strongest growth episodes in modern American history, especially in terms of tax revenue:

- In the years 1981–1983, that is, before the 1984 tax cuts, federal tax revenue grew at 5.4 percent per year.
- From 1984 and onward federal tax revenue grew at 8.7 percent per year.

Supply-side economists often also point to the tax cuts under Bush Jr. as further evidence that their theory is correct:

- In the years 2001–2003, federal tax revenue *decreased* by 4.1 percent per year.
- In the five following years, after the Bush tax cuts had been fully implemented, federal tax revenue *increased* by, on average, 7.4 percent per year.

The problem with supply-side theory is that it does not change the trajectory of government spending. Entitlement outlays are still determined by their own parameters, independent of whether taxes are high or low. Notably, neither President Reagan nor President Bush Jr. signed a balanced budget during their Oval Office tenures. Their reliance on supply-side economics may have paid off in terms of revenue growth, but they did not break the long-term negative trend in the federal budget.

From an ideological perspective, supply-side economics during the Reagan years was at best a half-way success. On the one hand, the tax cuts caused a surge in GDP growth and tax revenue, strong enough to eliminate the deficit caused by the tax cuts themselves. Thereby, millions of Americans were given an opportunity to become self-sufficient, even build a financial future for themselves that would shield them from ever having to depend on government for their livelihood.

On the other hand, the tax cuts left a larger deficit than what was there before the cuts – and again, there was no change in the modus operandi of the welfare state. Entitlements remained in place, available to everyone and anyone who qualified.

By preserving the entitlement programs, the Reagan administration left intact the key feature of the egalitarian institutions for economic redistribution. Since economic redistribution is the key for egalitarians toward their end goal – no economic differences – the net result of the Reagan tax cuts was to blow new life into a slowly imploding egalitarian project.

This does not mean that supply-side economics is ineffective against the welfare state's two economic problems. As mentioned, it inspired strong economic growth; as a result of that growth, it eventually reduced the deficit problem as well. The federal budget deficit declined toward the end of the Reagan years, and continued to do so during the Bush Sr. term. That was far from what supply-siders promised when the tax cuts were hashed out, but the long delay in bringing down the deficit is more attributable to continuous growth in entitlement spending than to the tax cuts themselves.

President Bush Jr. and his Republican friends in Congress repeated the Reagan administration's narrow focus on tax cuts. Consequently,

- In three of his eight years in office Bush allowed non-defense spending to grow at more than 7.5 percent per year;
- In only one year did non-defense spending grow at less than 4 percent per year;
- On average, non-defense spending expanded by 6.2 percent per year from 2001 to 2008.

Notes

1 The total data set includes 528 pairs of observations for the period 2002–2014, from Belgium, Denmark, Germany, Spain, France, Italy, Netherlands, Austria, Sweden, United Kingdom and Portugal. Data is selected solely based on availability from Eurostat. GDP growth, which is adjusted for inflation, is measured from same quarter previous year.
2 Tanner and Hughes (2014).
3 See http://ru.cbonds.info/news/item/472244 (accessed May 19, 2017) and http://ru.cbonds.info/news/item/478093 (accessed May 19, 2017).
4 See http://uk.reuters.com/article/2011/04/01/uk-ireland-idUKLDE7300KK20110401?pageNumber=2 (accessed May 19, 2017).
5 See www.bbc.co.uk/news/business-16552623 (accessed May 19, 2017).
6 See www.moodys.com/research/Moodys-downgrades-Frances-government-bond-rating-to-Aa1-from-Aaa—PR_260071 (accessed May 19, 2017).
7 See www.cnbc.com/id/100883386 (accessed May 19, 2017).
8 See www.huffingtonpost.com/2013/11/08/france-credit-rating-aa_n_4237916.html (accessed May 19, 2017).
9 See http://news.yahoo.com/p-cuts-credit-ratings-france-italy-spain-223152847.html (accessed May 19, 2017).
10 See http://sdw.ecb.europa.eu/servlet/desis?node=1000003501 (accessed May 19, 2017).
11 See www.businessinsider.com/citi-willem-buiter-spain-italy-need-sovereign-bailouts-2012-6 (accessed May 19, 2017).
12 See www.reuters.com/article/2014/03/10/eurozone-banks-idUSL6N0M717020140310 (accessed May 19, 2017).
13 See www.cnbc.com/2015/06/22/high-state-taxes-spurring-migration.html (accessed May 19, 2017) and https://mises.org/blog/census-data-shows-people-are-fleeing-high-tax-states (accessed May 19, 2017).
14 Mitchell (2012).
15 See, for example: https://danieljmitchell.wordpress.com/2013/11/04/iceland-switzerland-and-the-golden-rule-of-fiscal-policy/ (accessed May 19, 2017).
16 Larson (2016).
17 de Rugy (2012).
18 Alesina *et al.* (2014).
19 Alesina and de Rugy (2013).
20 See http://scholar.harvard.edu/files/alesina/files/austerity_in_09-13_2014.pdf (accessed May 19, 2017).

8

CONCLUSION

Egalitarianism has conquered America. Its impact on society, the economy, the culture and the mindset of the individual citizen is not yet quite as deep as it has been in Europe. Yet with the concessions from influential, supposedly non-egalitarian voices, resorting to fine-tuning the welfare state, it is apparent that a substantial segment of the opposition to egalitarianism has conceded defeat.

Perhaps it is their hope to solve the structural problems built into the welfare state. Perhaps they hope to do the work that egalitarians themselves seem to be unwilling to take on.

If so, their efforts deserve some recognition. Leading American egalitarians have repeatedly admitted that they do not even recognize the problem with slow growth; by logical consequence, they therefore also deny that the deficit problem has anything to do with the welfare state itself. If it is the intention of America's leading libertarian and conservative thinkers to fill the gap left by egalitarians on these issues, then their ambitions are respectable.

Provided, of course, that their work is placed in its proper context. Given the long European experience with slow growth, persistent deficits, austerity and even desperate monetary measures, it is extremely unlikely that even the cream of the crust among right-of-center thinkers in the United States can solve two of the welfare state's three pressing structural problems.

While placing these thinkers in their proper context, one should also not ignore the possibility that their work can avoid even bigger disasters than would follow if the welfare state, left unreformed, is allowed to pull America down into the depths of industrial poverty. In fact, once egalitarians wake up to the growth and deficit problems, they may return to the teachings of their intellectual forefathers. Gunnar Myrdal and John Kenneth Galbraith both saw increased government intervention into the economy as a way to prevent slow growth from eroding the fiscal sustainability of the welfare state. Their suggestions, various forms of economic planning, would bring about a systemic shift in the American economy.

If they did, it is more likely that they would align with John Kenneth Galbraith's softer stance on economic planning compared to Gunnar Myrdal's rather explicit support for Soviet-style teleological planning. In fact, Galbraith's work on this issue is deceptively tempting. The current American economic system, he said, is not very far from indicative planning. On the contrary, a modern industrialized economy is home to plenty of economic planning, with or without a large, redistributive government. In the foreword to the third edition of *The New Industrial State* Galbraith put the term "planning" to use in the context of a modern, industrialized economy:

> In earlier editions of this book I referred to the part of the economy that is dominated by great corporations as the *industrial system*. When I came to set this part of the economy in juxtaposition to the world of small firms – the market system – I found it did not serve. Small industrial firms could be subordinate to the market as large industrial firms are not. The phrase industrial system also has a connotation applicable to the whole of the modern economy. So, in *Economics and the Public Purpose*, I substituted the more accurately descriptive term *planning system* to describe the part of the modern bimodal economy that is dominated by the large corporations and where these, as an essential aspect of their planning, take markets under their control.

Later in the book (2010 ed., p. 997), he explains how the private planning system is extended to government in the form of three areas of central economic planning (numbers added):

> (1) The planning system has no inherent capacity for regulating total demand – for ensuring a supply of purchasing power sufficient to acquire what it produces. So it relies on the state for this. (2) At full employment there is no mechanism for holding prices and wages stable. This stabilization too is, or will one day become, an accepted function of the state. … (3) Finally, the planning system must rely on the state for trained and educated manpower, now a decisive factor of production.

This role of government is close to what the Myrdals prescribed in *The Demographic Crisis*, and what Gunnar Myrdal further elaborated in *Beyond the Welfare State*. Government is essential in maintaining full employment (the Myrdals) and a maximum of purchasing power (Galbraith). The latter is essential to the former, and both are essential to strong GDP growth.

Myrdal and Galbraith further agree on the expansion of government planning. Where Galbraith refers to price and wage planning as a means toward stabilizing the economy at full employment, Myrdal views planning of prices as a natural evolution of an increasingly sophisticated role of government in the modern economy (1958, pp. 46–50).

To further increase the likelihood that American egalitarians will return to a pro-growth agenda to save their welfare state, there are strong connections between growth-promoting arguments and Keynesian economic theory. A staple of global progressivism and liberalism, the macroeconomic theory developed by British economist John Maynard Keynes has been very influential for a good 80 years now. His globally reputable work was concentrated on the problem of why and how government can intervene with various fiscal measures when there is no hope of the private sector leading an economic recovery.

Later on, his contributions have led to the development of theories and fiscal-policy practices aiming to not only bring economies out of recessions, but also maintain growth and full employment over extended periods of time. Myrdal and Galbraith assign this more sophisticated role to government in the framework of the welfare state.

There are countless examples throughout the latter half of the twentieth century, from all over the world, of fiscal-policy episodes inspired by Keynesian theory. Economists have taken all kinds of positions on whether or not those episodes have been successful. A review of the literature would be redundant for the purposes of this book, though a substantial part of it gives egalitarians reason to believe that they can indeed save the welfare state from its own, built-in structural problems.

An egalitarian commitment to pro-growth policies, as defined by Myrdal, Galbraith and Keynes (or at least how Keynes is commonly interpreted by modern economists) would only add onto the role that government already plays in the economy. It would mean more economic-planning measures, more regulatory incursions, more government spending – and very probably not lower taxes.

There is another reason why one could expect an egalitarian commitment to traditional welfare-statist growth policies: they are well aligned with the moral hierarchy that gives ethical approval to the welfare state. In the egalitarian hierarchy, individual life is subordinate to the will of the state. Further expansion of government policies in line with prescriptions from primarily Myrdal and Galbraith would fall perfectly within the realm of that moral hierarchy.

It is important to recognize that the moral-hierarchy issue is not a problem isolated to egalitarians. It is also relevant to the right-of-center cavalry riding in to save the welfare state. By providing the egalitarian project with supply-side-derived growth policies, or any other policies designed to stimulate economic growth, they extend the fiscal life not only of the institutions of the welfare state but also its moral prime directive: life is instrumental to the egalitarian cause.

The only way that libertarians and conservatives would be able to avoid endorsing the egalitarian moral hierarchy is if they took measures to explicitly, and permanently, terminate spending programs designed for the purposes of economic redistribution. That, in turn, means terminating entitlement programs that, directly or indirectly, are responsible for approximately three quarters of federal government spending.

This is no small feat, but it is the only consistent response a libertarian can provide to the three structural problems of the welfare state. Anything less, any reforms to redistributive spending programs that perpetuate their existence, any tax policies that provide new funding for those programs are de facto egalitarian in nature.

The libertarian conquest of America may have slowed down in recent years, but it has not come to a halt. Its growing support in traditionally non-egalitarian circles suggests that it may just have paused to catch its breath and find its footing. Facing some resistance to its moral hierarchy, especially as put to work in health care, struggling through an economy that is barely growing and staggering under the federal government's massive debt, America's egalitarians may or may not be ready to solve these problems without help from new-found allies.

This is not a perspective that inspires much hope for the future. Failure to solve the welfare state's two economic problems will bring the U.S. economy to a grinding halt; failure to address its instrumental view of life will continue to erode the social, cultural and ethical standards that maintain a certain space of freedom in our society.

However, in lieu of a comprehensive alternative to egalitarianism, the best America can hope for is a coalition between egalitarians, conservatives and libertarians behind the banner of economic redistribution.

REFERENCES

Abramsky, S: The Battle Hymn of the War on Poverty; *The Nation*, January 15, 2014.

Aitken, Murray: *Impact of Cost-per-QALY Reimbursement Criteria on Access to Cancer Drugs*; IMS Institute for Healthcare Informatics; December 2014.

Alesina, A and de Rugy, V: There Is Good and Bad Austerity, and Italy Chose Bad; *Forbes Magazine*, March 7, 2013.

Alesina, A, Morgan, D, Boccia, R, Bourne, R, Howden, D, Melchiorre, M, de Rugy, V, Rohac, D and Marin, M: *Europe's Fiscal Crisis Revealed: An In-Depth Analysis of Spending, Austerity, and Growth*; Special Report #147; June 6, 2014; The Heritage Foundation.

Afonso, A, Schuknecht, L and Tanzi, V: *Public Sector Efficiency: An International Comparison*; Public Choice, Vol. 123, No. ¾ (June, 2005), 321–347.

Arjona, R, Ladaique, M and Pearson, M: Growth, Inequality and Social Protection, *Canadian Public Policy*, Vol. 29, Supplement (Jan. 2003), pp. S119–S139.

Babones, S: *Inequality and Growth*; Inequality.org, May 19, 2013. Available at: http://inequality.org/inequality-growth/ (accessed May 17, 2017).

Bartholomew, J: *The Welfare of Nations*; Cato Institute, Washington, DC 2016.

Beveridge, W: *Social Insurance and Allied Services;* Her Majesty's Stationery Office, London, UK 1942. Available at: www.bl.uk/collection-items/beveridge-report (accessed May 17, 2017).

Blau, J: Theories of the Welfare State; *Social Service Review*, Vol. 63, No. 1 (March 1989).

Boushey, H: *How Are Economic Inequality and Growth Connected?* Washington Center for Equitable Growth, Oct. 8, 2016. Available at: http://equitablegrowth.org/human-capital/economic-inequality-growth-connected/ (accessed May 17, 2017).

Califano, J: What Was Really Great About the Great Society? The Truths Behind the Conservative Myths; *The Washington Monthly*, October 1999.

Commager, H: *Lester Ward and the Welfare State*; Bobbs-Merrill, Indianapolis, IN 1967.

Cox, A: Does The Medical Profession Wish the National Health Insurance System to Continue?; *The British Medical Journal*, Vol. 2, No. 3171 (October 8, 1921) pp. 135–139.

de Rugy, Veronique: In Europe, Time for True Austerity; *Los Angeles Times*, May 18, 2012.

Edwards, Chris and de Rugy, Veronique: Earned Income Tax Credit: Small Benefits, Large Costs, *Tax and Budget Bulletin* No. 73, Cato Institute, October 16, 2015.

Emanuel, E and Battin, M: What Are the Potential Cost Savings from Legalizing Physician-Assisted Suicide? *New England Journal of Medicine*, Issue 339 (1998), pp. 167–172.

Erixon, Lennart: The Swedish Third Way: An Assessment of the Performance and Validity of the Rehn-Meidner Model; *Cambridge Journal of Economics*, Vol. 32, No. 3 (May 2008), pp. 367–393.

Erixon, Lennart: The Rehn-Meidner Model in Sweden: Its Rise, Challenges and Survival; *Journal of Economic Issues*, Vol. 44, No. 3 (September 2010), pp. 677–715.

Feeney, M: *Scrap the Welfare State and Give People Free Money*; Reason.com, November 26, 2013.

Fisher, Gordon: The Development and History of the Poverty Thresholds; *Social Security Bulletin*, Winter 1992.

Forbes, K: A Reassessment of the Relationship between Inequality and Growth, *The American Economic Review*, Vol. 90, No. 4 (September 2000), pp. 869–887.

Galbraith, James: *Inequality and Instability: A Study of the World Economy Just Before the Great Crisis*; Oxford University Press, Oxford, UK 2012.

Galbraith, John: *The Affluent Society*; Houghton-Mifflin, Boston, MA 1958.

Galbraith, John: *The New Industrial State*; Houghton-Mifflin, Boston, MA 1967.

Galbraith, John: *The Affluent Society and Other Writings*; The Library of America, New York, 2010.

Gallaway, L and Garrett, D: The Unintended Consequences of the War on Poverty; *The Cato Journal*, Winter 2016.

Gill, I and Raiser, M: Golden Growth: Restoring the Lustre of the European Economic Model; *Europe and Asia Studies*, World Bank. 2012.

Giubilini, A and Minerva, F: After-birth Abortion: Why Should the Baby Live? *Journal of Medical Ethics*, Vol. 39, No. 5 (May 2013), pp. 261–263.

Harris, H: British National Health Insurance Act of May 20, 1920; *Monthly Labor Review*, Vol. 11, No. 3 (September 1920), pp. 1–11.

Heckscher, G: *The Welfare State and Beyond*; University of Minnesota Press, Minneapolis, MN 1984.

Hirdman, Y: Social Engineering and the Woman Question: Sweden in the Thirties; *Studies in Political Economy* 44 (Summer 1994), pp. 73–94.

Kap, H: *Education and Citizenship in the Knowledge Society – Towards the Comparative Study of National Systems of Education*; Institute for Futures Studies, Stockholm, Sweden 2008.

Kap, H: *Reform of the Swedish Education System in the Post-war Period as Social Rights of Citizenship*; Conference paper, August 2009. Available at: www.cccg.umontreal.ca/rc19/pdf/kap-h_rc192009.pdf (accessed May 17, 2017).

Larson, S: *Remaking America: Welcome to the Dark Side of the Welfare State*; iUniverse, 2010.

Larson, S: *Ending the Welfare State: A Path to Limited Government that Won't Leave the Poor Behind*; Outskirts Press, Parker, CO 2012.

Larson, S: *Industrial Poverty: Yesterday Sweden, Today Europe, Tomorrow America*; Gower Applied Research, Farnham, UK 2014.

Larson, S: Balancing the Budget: Can the Swiss Debt Brake End Endless U.S. Deficits? *Journal of Governance and Regulation*, Vol. 5, Issue 4 (December 2016), pp. 99–105.

Leeson, R: Euthanasia Can be an Economic Decision Made Early; *San Francisco Chronicle*, October 11, 2013. Available at: www.sfgate.com/opinion/article/Euthanasia-can-be-an-economic-decision-made-early-4888933.php (accessed May 17, 2017).

Lindbeck, A: *Unemployment and Macroeconomics*; MIT Press, Cambridge, MA 1993.

Lindbeck, A, Molander, P, Persson, R, Petersson, O, Sandmo, A, Swedenborg, B and Thygesen, N: *Turning Sweden Around*; MIT Press, Cambridge, MA 1994.

Mitchell, D: *The Historical Lessons of Lower Tax Rates*; Backgrounder 1086, The Heritage Foundation (July 1996). Available at: www.heritage.org/research/reports/1996/07/bg1086nbsp-the-historical-lessons-of-lower-tax (accessed May 17, 2017).

Mitchell, D: How the Swiss 'Debt Brake' Tamed Government; *The Wall Street Journal*, April 25, 2012.
Murray, Charles: A Guaranteed Income for Every American; *The Wall Street Journal*, June 3, 2016.
Murray, M and Forstater, M (eds.): *The Job Guarantee: Toward True Full Employment*; Palgrave Macmillan, New York, NY 2013.
Myrdal, G: *An American Dilemma*; Harper and Row, New York, NY 1944.
Myrdal, G: *Beyond the Welfare State*; Duckworth, London, UK 1958.
Myrdal, G and Myrdal, A: *Kris i befolkningsfrågan [The Demographic Crisis]*; Albert Bonniers Förlag, Stockholm, Sweden 1934.
Neumann, P and Greenberg, D: Is the United States Ready for QALYs? *Health Affairs*, published online September 11, 2009; available at: http://content.healthaffairs.org/content/28/5/1366.full (accessed May 17, 2017).
Nozick, Robert: *Anarchy, State and Utopia*; Basic Books, New York, NY 1974.
Orient, Jane M: *Your Money* and *Your Life: The Price of "Universal Health Care,"* The Freeman, Foundation for Economic Education; December 2006.
Osborn, F: Development of a Eugenic Philosophy; *American Sociological Review*, Vol. 2, No. 3, June 1937.
Palier, B: *Hälso- och sjukvårdens reformer: en internationell jämförelse*; Sveriges Kommuner och Landsting, Stockholm, Sweden 2006. Available at: skl.se.
Persson, T and Tabellini, G: Is Inequality Harmful for Growth? *The American Economic Review*, Vol. 84, No. 3 (June 1994), pp. 600–621
Persson, U: *Value Based Pricing in Sweden: Lessons for Design?* Seminar Briefing #12, November 2012, Office of Health Economics; London, UK.
Pierson-Balik, Denise: Race, Class, and Gender in Punitive Welfare Reform: Social Eugenics and Welfare Policy; *Race, Gender and Class*, Volume 10, No. 1, 2003 (11–30).
Sewell, Dennis: How Eugenics Poisoned the Welfare State; *The Spectator*, November 25, 2009.
Spektorowski, A and Mizrachi, E: Eugenics and the Welfare State in Sweden: The Politics of Social Margins and the Idea of a Productive Society; *Journal of Contemporary History*, Vol. 39, No. 3 (July, 2004) pp. 333–352.
Stewart, E: British Health-Insurance System; *Monthly Labor Review*, Vol. 39, No. 4 (October 1934) pp. 823–846.
Strain, M: How to Cut Taxes and Help the Poor at the Same Time; *The Washington Post*, March 26, 2015. Available at: www.aei.org/publication/how-to-cut-taxes-and-help-the-poor-at-the-same-time/ (accessed May 17, 2017).
Tanner, M: *Leviathan on the Right*; Cato Institute, Washington, DC 2007. See especially Chapter 2.
Tanner, M and Hughes, C: *The Work versus Welfare Trade-Off: 2013*; Cato Institute White Paper; Washington, DC, August 2013.
Tanner, M and Hughes, C: War on Poverty Turns 50: Are We Winning Yet? *Policy Analysis* No. 761, Cato Institute, October 2014. Available at: www.cato.org/publications/policy-analysis/war-poverty-turns-50-are-we-winning-yet (accessed May 17, 2017).
Tanner, M, Moore, S and Hartman, D: *The Work versus Welfare Trade-Off: An Analysis of the Total Level of Benefits by State*; Cato Institute, September 1995.
Trattner, Walter: *From Poor Law to Welfare State*; 6th ed.; The Free Press, New York, NY 1999.
Zwolinski, M: The Libertarian Case for a Basic Income; Libertarianism.org, December 5, 2013. Available at: www.libertarianism.org/columns/libertarian-case-basic-income (accessed May 17, 2017).

INDEX

Abortion 66-70, 127; and eugenics 66; infanticide 67-70
Affordable Care Act 14, 52-3, 56, 72; and NFIB v. Sebelius 56
Austrian economic theory 113

Bartholomew, James 13
Basic income guarantee 97, 99
Beveridge, Lord 10, 49-50, 54
Beveridge Report 49-50, 54, 62
Boushey, Heather 86
Budget 3, 8; federal 3;
Buiter, Willem 113
Bush Jr., George W 6, 8, 20, 58, 115
Business cycle 25, 42-3, 95, 110

Central economic planning *see* Planning
Clinton, Bill 15, 53, 57, 85
Clinton, Hillary 2, 86-7, 119-21
COLA *see* Cost of Living Adjustments
Common core 36
Conservatism 2, 6-7, 10-11, 15; social 6-7, 11
Conservative 2-11, 20, 28-9, 49, 51-2, 58, 83, 87, 118-19; and Beveridge Report 49
Cost benefit analysis 64
Cost of Living Adjustment 16

De Rugy, Veronique 118-19
Deficit 9, 25, 49, 58, 70, 82, 84, 95, 102-07, 110, 112-21; chronic 9, 102; and economic stagnation 104; GDP ratio 103; as permanent funding source 58, 105, 112; and slow growth 84; structural 9
Debt *see* Government debt

Earned Income Tax Credit 16-18, 20, 52, 89-92
Economic growth 6, 8-9, 15, 18, 20-4, 27, 31-3, 35, 44-5, 47, 58, 62, 66, 79-100, 102-03, 105-07, 109-11, 114-15, 118-23
Economic Opportunity Act 6, 16, 55
Education 28, 32-8, 45, 52, 68; and national curriculum 35-7, 68; policy 32-7, 68; and uniform system 34-37
Egalitarian project 3, 6-8, 18, 22-3, 29, 33-4, 47-58, 66, 77, 80-1, 107, 116, 119-20
Egalitarianism 2-3; 5-12, 15-18, 20-4, 28-31, 33, 40, 44, 47-58, 60-1, 67-8, 73, 76-8, 84, 87, 98, 99, 105, 111-12, 122, 125; absolute 7, 10-11, 22-4, 28, 30-1, 40, 44, 47-9, 51-2, 55; and basic income guarantee 99
EITC *see* Earned Income Tax Credit
Entitlements 3, 5, 15-17, 20-1, 28-9, 50, 60, 66-8, 70, 87-9, 93, 95, 102, 105-06,

111-12, 117, 120
Equality 18, 36, 50, 84; income 84, 87; in opportunity 36, 50; in outcome 50
Eugenics 30-1, 58, 60-78; fiscal 58, 60-78
Europe 1-3, 5, 8-9, 16, 22, 28-9, 48-9, 51-2, 55-7, 61, 65, 69, 75, 79, 81-3, 93-4, 102, 104-07, 109, 111-19
Euthanasia 64, 72

Fabian Society 61-3, 65
Food stamps *see* Supplementary Nutritional Assistance Program

Galbraith, James 23, 83, 95-7
Galbraith, John 23, 29, 55, 83-4, 89, 103, 118-19, 122-24
GDP *see* Gross Domestic Product
GDP growth *see* Economic growth
Giubilini, Alberto 67-70
Government 5-6, 8, 10-11, 15-17, 21-5, 27-8, 30, 32, 34-5, 37-45, 47-52, 56, 58, 61-70, 73-7, 79, 84-7, 92, 98-9, 102-14, 116-20, 123-24; spending 5-6, 8, 10-11, 15-17, 20, 22, 30, 55, 67, 70, 75, 83-4, 87-9, 97, 102-07, 109-21, 124-25
Gross Domestic Product 1, 20-1, 27, 31, 33, 35, 43-4, 47, 57, 66, 72, 80-5, 87-9, 94-7, 102-03, 107, 109-10, 116, 120, 123

Haushaltsunwertes Leben 65
Health care 3, 5, 15, 22, 24, 28, 31, 37-40, 45, 50, 52, 56-7, 65-77, 79, 85, 105, 110, 112, 125; and eugenics 31, 65-7, 69-76; and palliative care 71, 73; single payer 22, 37-40, 50, 52, 56-7, 66, 70, 73-4, 105, 117
Heckscher, Gunnar 29, 56
Hirdman, Yvonne 34
Housing 3, 5, 27-8, 35, 40-5, 81, 96; credits 27, 43, 96; policy 27, 42-3; standards 27, 41-2; subsidies 3, 5, 27, 40, 42-3

Income 7-8, 10, 16-24, 27-30, 33-4, 39, 42, 44, 50, 53-4, 56, 60, 66, 79, 84-7, 90-7, 99, 105-06, 122; differences 7, 16, 22-23, 30, 39, 84-7, 94, 96; equality 84, 86-7, 96; tax 8, 17-18, 20-1, 24, 28-9, 60, 81-2, 86, 90-3, 99, 105
Income redistribution *see* Redistribution

Jefferson, Thomas 33
Johnson, Lyndon 2, 6, 10-14, 29, 47, 54-5, 85

Kennedy, John 55, 85
Keynes, John Maynard 124
Keynesian economic theory 109

Laffer curve 85, 92
Lebensunwertes leben 74
Liverpool Care Pathway 71-2

Medicaid 3, 5, 12, 14-15, 92, 110
Medicare 3, 6, 12, 58, 72, 98-9, 104
Meidner, Rudolf 24, 26
Minerva, Francesca 67-70
Mitchell, Dan 117
Myrdal, Alva 10, 22-4, 27, 30-5, 37, 40, 43, 45, 49, 65-6, 73, 75-6, 119
Myrdal, Gunnar 10, 22-4, 27, 30-5, 27-40, 42-4, 48-52, 55-6, 61-3, 65-6, 73, 75-6, 81-2, 84, 103, 118-19, 122-24

Nozick, Robert 8, 98

Orshansky, Mollie 16, 55
Osborn, Frederic 65

Paul, Rand 5

QALY *see* Quality Adjusted Life Years
Quality Adjusted Life Years 73-4, 76-8
Palliative care *see* Health care
Parliamentary democracy 50-2
Personal Responsibility and Work Opportunity Act 53, 64
Planning 23-8, 30-4, 40-1, 42, 48-9, 52, 55, 61, 81, 103, 123-24; central economic 23-8, 41, 43, 48-9, 52, 55, 81, 103, 123-24; indicative 48, 55, 123; Soviet style 48-9, 123; teleological 55, 123
Population stock 30-2, 34, 61-2, 75-76
Poverty 6-8, 10-17, 29, 49, 55, 90, 96, 98, 100, 104, 122; absolute 7-8, 11, 14-17, 55, 96; Elizabethan laws of 10; industrial 100, 104, 122; relative 7-8, 14-17, 29, 55, 96; war on 2-3, 6-7, 10-13, 16-17, 20, 23, 29, 47, 50, 52, 54-6, 87, 119

PRWORA *see* Personal Responsibility and Work Opportunity Act

Reagan, Ronald 6, 8-10, 20, 58, 85, 87, 115, 119-21
Redistribution 6, 8, 10, 16-18, 20-3, 29, 32-4, 47, 49-1, 53-4, 70, 78, 84-7, 89-90, 93-5, 97, 99
Rehn, Gösta 24, 26
Rehn-Meidner model 24-7, 29, 47-8, 55, 63, 66, 80-1
Ryan, Paul 90

Sanders, Bernie 2, 18, 85
SCHIP *see* State Children's Health Insurance Program
Sewell, Dennis 61
SNAP *see* Supplemental Nutritional Assistance Program
State Children's Health Insurance Program 57
Supplemental Nutritional Assistance Program 3, 5, 12-15, 17, 92, 98

TANF *see* Temporary Assistance to Needy Families
Tanner, Michael 13, 98
Tax 5-6, 8, 16-18, 20-1, 24-8, 31-2, 35, 37, 43-5, 47, 56, 60, 66-7, 69, 75-6, 79-82, 86, 89-93, 95, 102, 104-05, 111-12, 114-21; cuts 6, 8, 20, 67, 115, 118, 120-21; on income 17-18, 20, 28, 81-2, 89-93, 105; marginal 18, 21, 90-3, 99; revenue 8, 20, 24, 31-2, 35, 37, 43, 48, 62, 66, 69-72, 75-6
Temporary Assistance to Needy Families 3, 5, 81-83, 95, 102-05, 110-12, 114, 117, 120
Thatcher, Margaret 28
Trattner, William 9-10
Trump, Donald 2-3, 6, 56, 58, 114-15, 119-20

Unions 25-6; and wage negotiations 25
Universal basic income *see* Basic income guarantee

Wages 25-7, 39, 47, 81, 102, 123; minimum 5, 12; negotiations 25
Welfare state 1-11, 16, 18, 20-45, 47-54, 56-8, 60-3, 65-78, 80-5, 89-90, 93, 95, 97-100, 102-07, 109, 111-21, 123-25; American 2, 6, 8-10, 16, 20-45, 50, 52, 54, 57-8, 84, 86, 105, 111, 114-15, 118; British 2, 38-9, 49-50, 54, 62; Swedish 2, 10, 20-45, 47-50, 54, 56, 62, 80-2; exogenous theory of 82-5
Welfare state reform 3, 5, 13, 24, 64, 100, 115, 118, 122, 125